Teaching and Learning Multiliteracies

CHANGING TIMES, CHANGING LITERACIES

Michèle Anstey
Geoff Bull

AUSTRALIAN LITERACY
EDUCATORS' ASSOCIATION
416 Magill Road
Kensington Gardens, SA, 5068, Australia
www.alea.edu.au

INTERNATIONAL
Reading Association
800 BARKSDALE ROAD, PO BOX 8139
NEWARK, DE 19714-8139, USA
www.reading.org

The International Reading Association attempts, through its publications, to provide a forum for a wide spectrum of opinions on reading. This policy permits divergent viewpoints without implying the endorsement of the Association.

Director of Publications Dan Mangan
Editorial Director, Books and Special Projects Teresa Curto
Managing Editor, Books Shannon T. Fortner
Acquisitions and Developmental Editor Corinne M. Mooney
Associate Editor Charlene M. Nichols
Associate Editor Elizabeth C. Hunt
Production Editor Amy Messick
Books and Inventory Assistant Rebecca A. Fetterolf
Permissions Editor Janet S. Parrack
Assistant Permissions Editor Tyanna L. Collins
Production Department Manager Iona Muscella
Supervisor, Electronic Publishing Anette Schütz
Senior Electronic Publishing Specialist R. Lynn Harrison
Electronic Publishing Specialist Lisa M. Kochel
Proofreader Stacey Lynn Sharp

Project Editor Elizabeth C. Hunt

Cover Design, Linda Steere; Photos © Clipart.com except the following: © Creatas—girl using laptop and boy using microscope (top left), children holding globe (center); children holding paper suns (center right); © Photodisc—students singing (top right), boys reading (bottom left), young children on laptop (center left).

Copyright 2006 by the International Reading Association, Inc., and the Australian Literacy Educators' Association. Published in cooperation with the Australian Literacy Educators' Association, 416 Magill Road, Kensington Gardens, SA, 5068, Australia.

Web addresses in this book were correct as of the publication date but may have become inactive or otherwise modified since that time. If you notice a deactivated or changed Web address, please e-mail books@reading.org with the words "Website Update" in the subject line. In your message, specify the Web link, the book title, and the page number on which the link appears.

Library of Congress Cataloging-in-Publication Data
Anstey, Michèle.
  Teaching and learning multiliteracies : changing times, changing literacies / Michèle Anstey and Geoff Bull.
     p. cm.
  Includes bibliographical references and index.
  ISBN-13: 978-0-87207-586-3
  1. Reading (Elementary) 2. Visual literacy--Study and teaching (Elementary) 3. Media literacy--Study and teaching (Elementary) I. Bull, Geoff. II. Title.
  LB1573.A63 2006
  372.4--dc22
                                                                                              2006011578

In memory of my father,
Harry George Victor Ward (George) 1922–2005.
He truly understood and valued the importance of literacy and education
and inspired my love of both.
—Michèle

In memory of my mother,
Lilian Maud Bull 1919–2004.
She may not have written the words, but she played an important part
in the formation of my thoughts and ideas about literacy.
—Geoff

CONTENTS

The purpose of this book is to introduce the concept of *multiliteracies*, a term first widely used by the New London Group (1996) and later explored in more detail by Cope and Kalantzis (2000). The theory of multiliteracies draws upon a range of new ideas about new literacies that have been brought about by technological change and the globalisation of economies. The strength of the theory is that it balances new ideas about literacy with more established ideas by being situated in successful practice from current and previous approaches. While exploring this balance, teachers will be introduced to the language necessary to talk about these new literacies with their students. The aim is not to introduce unnecessary jargon but rather to provide the required metalanguage to address these emerging concepts.

The intended audience for this book is those teachers who are involved in the teaching and learning of literacy with students ages 5 to 12, that is, those in elementary, or primary, school. However, multiliteracies offer much that can be useful to teachers of older students up to age 15, particularly those involved in middle school education and the seamless transition from elementary to secondary school. Teachers in schools will benefit from a well-argued theory about multiliteracies in addition to well-developed and well-thought-out practices. If a practice works, then that is because it has a well-thought-out theoretical base. Conversely, a good theory must be able to be translated into good practice.

Consequently, this text outlines theoretical issues and presents a range of practical suggestions in order to achieve this balance. First, a number of Reflection Strategies are intended to focus teachers' attention on the issues that underlie the theory. Within these strategies are some practical activities designed to assist in the exploration of the theory. The Reflection Strategies appear only in chapters 1, 2, and 4 because those chapters contain new understandings about literacy, multiliteracies, and texts. In chapters 3–6, the focus moves from theory toward planning, pedagogy, and practice with multiliteracies. Throughout the book, the Theory Into Practice: Classroom Application sections encourage thinking about the classroom application of multiliteracies. These sections contain practical examples of activities to implement at the classroom or school level. These two specialised features are designed to bridge what is sometimes seen as a gap between theory and practice.

Chapter 1 outlines the conditions, at local and global levels, that led to the need for new literacies, particularly multiliteracies. These conditions, although they operate largely outside the classroom, need to be clearly understood. Otherwise, multiliteracies will be seen merely as the current bandwagon or latest fashion rather than as a necessary development resulting from technological, cultural, and societal change. This approach is not simply the latest trend, which can be either adopted or ignored, but rather is essential if teachers and schools are to remain relevant to, and useful in, students' lives.

After the conditions that led to the development of multiliteracies have been explored, the focus turns to defining multiliteracies. Chapter 2 explores new concepts about text, introduces the Four Resource Model, and incorporates discussions about the range of semiotic systems that form the foundations of the new texts.

Chapter 3 explores the pedagogies that have developed to promote and support teaching and learning multiliteracies. This chapter makes a strong case for an emphasis on explicit teaching with a particular focus on the role of teacher talk, the structure of lessons, and the materials teachers should use.

Chapter 4 focuses on the use of children's literature as a way of initially exploring multiliteracies. Children's literature provides an ideal base from which to launch into new forms of text and the new literacies, and particularly the special qualities of postmodern picture books lend themselves to introducing students of all ages to multiliteracies. New trends in children's literature, particularly the postmodern picture book, are examined in chapter 4.

Chapter 5 examines still and moving images and suggests that exploring the codes and conventions of these images provides a starting point for teachers or schools that want to move away from an overreliance on print texts.

Chapter 6 presents a number of tools that can be used to address the question of balance in planning. The relationship of guided reading, outcomes-based curricula, the integrated curriculum, and schoolwide approaches to planning are also explored.

As the authors of this book, we hope that it encourages you to explore multiliteracies further and that it proves to be as exciting a journey for you as it has been for us and the teachers with whom we have worked.

We wish to thank the colleagues, teachers, and students with whom we have worked over the years, in particular the staff at Fairview Heights State School, Toowoomba, who have worked with us in the area of multiliteracies over the last two years. The Literate Futures Team of Education Queensland and coordinators of The Learning Development Centres (Literacy) with whom we have worked closely since 2001 have also contributed much through collegial work and discussion. All of you have taught us that in order to develop understandings and knowledge that are likely to be remembered, used, and transformed it is necessary to investigate for yourself and discuss and reflect with others.

Thanks also to the staff of the International Reading Association who have assisted in the production of this work.

 **Michèle Anstey** is co-director of ABC: Anstey and Bull Consultants in Education and conducts professional development in literacy and children's literature throughout Australia. She also serves as a consultant to state and private education systems.

Michèle was an associate professor at the University of Southern Queensland, where she taught undergraduate and postgraduate courses and supervised doctoral research. During her academic career, she was deputy dean of the faculty of education, won the University Award for Excellence in Scholarship, and received a National Award for Excellence in Practice, Design and Delivery of Open and Distance Learning.

Michèle was director of and principal adviser to the Literate Futures Project for Education Queensland, a statewide professional development initiative for all teachers. As part of this project, she authored *Literate Futures: Reading* (Education Queensland, 2002) and *Professional Development: The Teaching of Reading in a Multiliterate World: A Handbook* (Education Queensland, 2004). In 2004, she was a consultant to the Queensland Years 1–10 English Syllabus.

Michèle is also a former editor of the *Australian Journal of Language and Literacy* and has been an active member of the Darling Downs Council of the Australian Literacy Educators' Association.

She has taught in the states of Victoria, New South Wales, and Queensland in country and city schools and state and private systems. She retains a keen interest in rural schooling from these experiences and her own early school life. Her research interests are literacy teaching practices, multiliteracies, children's literature, and visual literacy.

Michèle gained her initial teaching qualification at Canberra University (Canberra, ACT), her MEd (Hons) at University of New England (Armidale, NSW), and her PhD at Griffith University (Brisbane, Qld).

 **Geoff Bull** is co-director of ABC: Anstey and Bull Consultants in Education. He works with teachers and education systems throughout Australia in professional development contexts.

Geoff was an associate professor at the University of Southern Queensland, where he was a program head and taught undergraduate and postgraduate courses in literacy and children's literature. He founded the Language and Literacy Research Unit and developed the first postgraduate courses in children's literature and has supervised research in these areas. He won the University Award for Excellence in Research and has received several national research grants.

Geoff is a former national president of the Australian Literacy Educators' Association and founding member of the Australian Literacy Federation (ALF). His contribution to the Australian Literacy Educators' Association (formerly Australian Reading Association) has been recognised by the Award of the Inaugural Medal for Excellence in leadership, administration, and promotion of the association. He is also on the editorial board of the *Australian Journal of Language and Literacy*.

Geoff was also an author for the Literate Futures Project for Education Queensland, and in 2004 he was a consultant to the Queensland Years 1–10 English Syllabus.

Formerly a teacher and teacher librarian in state schools throughout country Queensland, Geoff is particularly interested in community literacies and rural education as well as speculative fiction and postmodern trends in children's literature.

Geoff gained an initial teaching qualification at University of Queensland (Brisbane, Qld), his MEd at University of Queensland, and his MLitt and PhD at University of New England (Armidale, NSW).

Michèle Anstey and Geoff Bull have published *The Literacy Landscape* (Pearson Education Australia, 2005), *The Literacy Labyrinth* (2nd Edition; Pearson Education Australia, 2004); *The Literacy Lexicon* (2nd Edition; Pearson Education Australia, 2003); *Crossing the Boundaries* (Pearson Education Australia, 2002), and *Reading the Visual: Written and Illustrated Children's Literature* (Harcourt Australia, 2000).

If you would like to correspond with the authors, they can be contacted by e-mail at anstey.bull@bigpond.com.

CHAPTER 1

Changing Times, Changing Literacies

n order to understand the term *multiliteracies* and its role in the teaching and learning of literacy, it is necessary to explore the concept of literacy. Part of this exploration includes developing an understanding of the influence of social, technological, and economic change on literacy. The focus of this chapter is to reflect on common literate practices, in other words, the ways people have used literacy in the past and present as part of their social, cultural, working, leisure, and civic lives. From these reflections, teachers and students can extrapolate the knowledge, skills, and processes about literacy that are required in order to operate successfully as citizens of the local and global community in the present and future. That is, they can begin to understand how they use literacy differently for different purposes and that knowledge, skills, and understandings about literacy have to be deep and flexible in order for them to use literacy successfully across all parts of their lives. Knowing this, teachers can develop appropriate pedagogies to ensure their students have literate futures.

The world continues to change in technological, social, and economic ways. As a result, the texts we use continue to change, the ways we use literacy will change as purposes and contexts change, and literacy knowledge, skills, and processes will continue to change. The literate person must be able to combine and recombine existing and new literacy knowledge, skills, and purposes for new purposes and new contexts using new technologies. Therefore, the ways we teach and learn literacy will need to change.

Change as the New Constant

Change is an overarching characteristic of the later 20th and early 21st centuries and will likely continue to be so. Change affects all aspects of teachers' and students' lives, from the global to the local, and is realised in workplace and leisure activities. It is so influential that life in the 21st century is often referred to as *new times*. Because workplace, leisure, social,

1

cultural, and civic environments are changing as people deal with globalisation and technological advances, the ways people practice literacy are also changing. Consequently, the teaching and learning of literacy need to change. Students not only need a broader knowledge base about texts and literacy; they also need the resources, attitudes, and strategies to adjust to and develop responsive and appropriate literate practices when necessary. They need to be able to cope with changing times and changing literacies.

Workplace Change and Globalisation

Workplace change and globalisation require different literate practices to those that were predominant in the period immediately following World War II. As A. Luke and Freebody (2000) suggest,

> Being a child, being an adolescent and, indeed, becoming literate, have changed in some fundamental ways. The tool kit of basic skills that served many of us well in the 1950s is inadequate today. (p. 7)

The 1950s-style literacy toolkit referred to by Luke and Freebody was largely concerned with the technologies of print on paper, that is, reading and writing words. Although some texts had illustrations, diagrams, and photographs, the teaching and learning focus was on interpreting the one meaning of the printed word, with little attention given to the role, or the reading, of the illustrative or diagrammatic text. Similarly, the influence of page layout on meaning was all but ignored. This basic, print-dominated literacy toolkit suited a world in which jobs were secure, were usually held for life, and required only basic literacy skills with the technologies of the day: pen and paper, or typewriter and paper. Workplaces at this time were largely hierarchical, and each person had a specialised set of tasks that required a specific set of literacy skills. Therefore, people seldom needed to complete tasks that required a broader range of literacy skills or the adaptation and use of current skills in new ways.

Because workplaces were largely hierarchical in structure, only people in higher or executive positions would normally interact with interstate or international clients, largely through phone or letter and only occasionally travelling to meet person to person. There was little pressure to understand much about other cultures and how social and cultural practices might affect communication and negotiation, because there was less globalised business. For people conducting international business, the communication and travel technologies meant that they rarely had to deal with clients and colleagues face to face.

Globalisation and the increasing use of digital technology have had great effect on workplaces and working lives and consequently on the literate practices necessary to succeed in the workplace (New London Group, 1996). Many corporate workplaces in fast capitalist (i.e., consumer- and multinational-driven) cultures such as Australia and the United States have moved to a less hierarchical organisation in which teamwork and multiskilling, or having multiple skills, are valued (Cope & Kalantzis, 1995). In other words, employees are required to do other people's jobs when they are away, to work together as a team on tasks, collaborate, strategise, and problem solve in order to get the job done. Simply being able to read and write effectively is only one set of literacy skills necessary to these workplaces. The ability to communicate orally, listen productively and critically, negotiate, use higher order thinking skills, and cooperate are some of the other literacy skills now required. Being able to access and use new technology and to identify people with specialised skills and work with them as part of a team are also important characteristics of the new worker. The 1950s toolkit is simply not enough for workers today. Certainly many of its tools are still necessary, but they are not sufficient.

REFLECTION
STRATEGY

Reflect on the collaborative nature of many workplace tasks and the way we draw upon skills from different parts of our lives in order to complete them.

1. Identify a task that you recently completed that required collaborative work. How did the group organise itself to get the task done?

2. Did some participants have specialised knowledge or expertise, and how and when did they participate?

3. Apart from knowledge and skills necessary to the actual task, what other expertise and knowledge were needed? For example, did someone take on a leadership role, a coaching role, an organisation role?

4. How were differences of opinion or action resolved? If they did not occur, why do you think this was the case?

5. Was anyone in the group silenced or marginalised, and, if so, how and why did this happen? Did anyone dominate? How and why did this happen?

6. What was the effect of the marginalisation or domination on the overall task completion and working atmosphere?

7. Think about the literate practices that were required here that went beyond specific knowledge about the task. When and how did you learn them?

Changes in the nature of workplaces are not limited to industry and corporate business. Rural occupations require higher levels of literacy as technology and environmental protection influence agronomy, or scientific agriculture. Farm machinery is often computerised and programmed using global positioning technology to enable the most efficient ploughing and planting of seed for maximum yield. For example, in cotton-growing areas in Queensland, Australian farmers are required to have their fields levelled using global positioning systems to minimise the runoff of chemicals into the water table. These farmers are also using the global positioning system with the computers in their tractors to ensure that the tractors always travel the same paths. That way, the tractor compacts the same soil rather than the planting area, which would impede growth. Farmers also use the information to ensure that seed drilling occurs in exactly the same place for each crop. This strategy increases the crop's yield because the roots are able to grow more easily in already loosened soil. The use of this equipment is changing the nature of these farmers' workplaces. Clearly the people selling, maintaining, and using the global positioning systems and computer equipment need to be technologically literate, but they also need to be able to conduct conversations with their rural clients, who may not have high levels of technological literacy, to ensure that the clients' needs are understood and met.

Another change in the workplace is the increasing demand for certification in jobs that were once considered blue-collar and therefore appropriate for those with poor literacy skills. For example, in the rural sector, certification to mix and use chemicals is now required, and therefore higher levels of literacy are needed to obtain that certification. So-called blue-collar jobs are no longer the province of those with poor literacy skills. For example, a middle-aged worker on a cotton farm in Queensland, Australia, who left school at age 15 and went straight to labouring work on the farm, was the most senior worker and therefore had been mixing the chemicals and monitoring water use on the farm for some years. Regulations now require that he obtain certification to continue this job. In order to obtain the certification, he has to attend night classes at the local technical college, read texts, and sit for exams. Therefore, his current literacy skills must be expanded to obtain certification.

Trends in occupations and employment indicate that in the 21st century most workers will have a greater number and range of occupations in their working lives. Changes in occupation may mean not only a change of workplace but also moving to a new town, state or province, or country, and encountering social and cultural changes in home, leisure, community, and workplace. Such moves and changes in occupation may require flexibility and strategic thinking as the acquisition and application of new literate practices are required in every aspect of one's life.

Explore concepts about what literate practices are, the role of literate practices in your life, how technology influences literate practices, and the concept of literacy as dynamic rather than static.

1. Draw a table to represent a timeline of your life. In the first column, identify the decades of your life. In the next column, list a few of the literate practices you used in home, leisure, workplace, social, cultural, religious, or civic activities. This would include listening, speaking, reading, writing, or viewing. In the next column write the purpose for that practice and the context: Why did you do it, what were you trying to achieve, where were you? In the final column list the technologies you used (e.g., pen and paper, typewriter, computer, phone, mobile phone). A sample decade has been completed as an example.

Timeline of Literate Practices

Decade	Literate Practices	Purpose and Context	Technology Used
1970–1980	Listening to music	Pleasure, home	Tape recorder and record player
	Presenting a seminar	Assessment, university	Voice plus overhead projector
	Working out my budget	Balancing income and expenses, home	Calculator, pen and paper
	Talking to bank officer and reading pamphlet	Applying for loan for car	Listening, speaking, reading, paper
	Reading newspaper rental ads and town map	Looking for somewhere to live near work that is affordable	Reading paper and print, maps
	Watching the news coverage of Vietnam War	Keeping up with current events, home	Television, listening and viewing
	Working out game strategy for hockey	Leisure, local sport field clubroom	Listening and speaking, chalkboard and chalk

2. Looking at your timeline, reflect upon the following:

- How did your literate practices change over time?
- Did you need to learn new practices and, if so, why (e.g., change of occupation, technology)?
- Do you use some of the same literate practices for a range of purposes and in different contexts? If so, how and why? For example, in the sample, would listening and speaking about the car loan be the same as the listening and speaking about the hockey strategy?
- Consider how the literate practices listed in the sample would look in the current decade. What would change? Would it be only the technology? What would you need to know and be able to do now that you did not then?

3. Having completed this task, think about the following questions:

- What are literate practices?
- Where do we engage in literate practices, and why? What is their role in our lives?
- How do our literate practices change depending on purpose and context?
- How has technology influenced our literate practices?

THEORY INTO PRACTICE: CLASSROOM APPLICATION

The following questions and activities relate to the concepts explored in the previous Reflection Strategy. They challenge you to consider the implications for your pedagogy and teaching practices.

Activity 1
Use this activity to expand the focus of your pedagogy so that students can understand how literacy works and have the knowledge and understanding they need to cope with changing literate practices, technologies, and contexts.

1. Ask your students to complete a timeline similar to the one you completed. If you have very young students who are not yet writing, you could jointly construct one timeline for the class using pictures and words.
2. Compare your timeline with theirs and talk about the similarities and differences. Initial discussions might be about old technologies and new technologies and how life has changed, even in your students' life-

times. Use this discussion to focus on how we need to continually learn new literate practices as our lives and technologies change.

3. Focus your discussion on the ways in which we use literate practices and technologies differently depending on purpose and context. Choose a few examples from your students' timelines to see if you can work out exactly how the purpose and context change the practices.

4. See if you and the students can identify what you would need to know and be able to do in order to achieve your purpose successfully in each context. The idea here is to help your students understand that it is not enough simply to be able to read and understand the words. You must also be able to conduct the conversation necessary or apply the knowledge from the reading appropriately to achieve the purpose. So part of being literate is to have the appropriate social behaviours for the context and to be able to use your knowledge and skills in new and different ways.

Activity 2

While planning a literacy lesson, use these questions to inform your planning to prepare students to cope with changing literacies. You should also use the questions to reflect upon your lessons.

1. Did you discuss why you were teaching your students this new skill?

2. Did you discuss how and where the skill might be used in everyday settings outside school?

3. Did you talk about the knowledge and skills the students already had that would help them with this task?

4. Did you ask students to use the knowledge they had to predict how they might attempt this task and identify what else they needed to know in order to do it?

Technological Change, Social Change, and Globalisation

Another significant aspect of change that affects literacy and literate practices is technology and the way it connects people to their local community, state or province, country, and global world. People participate in global events either directly or vicariously via technology. Not everyone can fly to different parts of the world and experience other cultures, but they can all view distant areas via various media platforms (e.g., television, mobile phones with video and photo capabilities, video cameras). Digital technologies and satellites beam these events directly into our lounge rooms or handheld mobile phones and computers. Thus, we can see in real time events actually unfolding, be they war, sporting events, or natural disasters such as volcanic explosions or floods.

Viewers need to remember, however, that what they see is a selected, or edited, version of what is happening, governed by who is filming, their beliefs and views about what is happening, their cultural or workplace allegiances, and what or how much they are allowed to film and send. The final product may also have been further editorialised and shaped by the addition of commentary, music, or sound effects. Students will need to recognise that technology is manipulated and used by people, and therefore nothing they see or hear is neutral. The message is shaped by a range of people who are influenced by everything from their beliefs to the time allocated for the completed message. Then, once people read or view the technology, their interpretations of the messages are influenced by their beliefs, backgrounds, and knowledge. This point is particularly important to consider when using the Internet. Students should consider the origin, purpose, authenticity, and authority of the person, group, or business that has set up a website when they are viewing its content.

REFLECTION
STRATEGY

Consider how technology has made the world smaller, changed the ways you work and practice literacy, potentially influenced your views of the world, and brought you into contact with a wide range of social, cultural, religious, and ethnic groups. Review some of the main articles in a selection of local, state or province, and national daily newspapers available in your community. In each case try to determine whether the issues or events that are being reported on reflect local, national, or global concerns.

1. What are the proportions of local, state, national, and global news in each of them? Compare these proportions across the newspapers.

2. Review articles that report on ethnic, cultural, or religious unrest and compare the way different newspapers report. What are the differences between local, state, and national reporting?

3. How much is reported through words and how much through images, diagrams, tables, and so forth?

4. Compare these newspaper reports with the representations of the same issues or events in another form of media (e.g., local or national television, radio, the Internet).

Because people are now privy to global events through technology and multimedia, they have become more aware of global trends. For example, people everywhere have seen the breakdown of amalgamated states such as the USSR in Europe into individual nations characterised by religious, ethnic, and cultural affiliations. Media audiences have seen similar trends in Asia and the Pacific, manifested in the unrest of the Philippines, Indonesia, Fiji, and the Solomon Islands. More recently people around the world have seen, heard about, and experienced acts of terror perpetrated by people with particular values and beliefs about world events and religion. What readers and viewers see and understand about these events can influence their day-to-day literate practices in different settings. They may view a social, cultural, or ethnic group differently, and then change their behaviour—their ways of speaking and interacting with the group members—in positive or negative ways. Given the multicultural aspects of many workplaces, this may mean that work is conducted in different ways.

REFLECTION
STRATEGY

Think about how your encounters with different cultural groups are mediated and whether your attitudes and behaviour are modified by the cultural groups with whom you are interacting. Consider the range of social, cultural, religious, and ethnic groups you have come into contact with today or during the last few days.

1. Where have you encountered these groups or individuals? Has it been in person or via electronic means (e.g., phone, e-mail, or Internet)?

2. Was this encounter in a leisure (e.g., viewing a television program or movie), workplace, business, community, or social setting?

3. Did the social, cultural, religious, or ethnic characteristics of these people influence the way you communicated or behaved? For example, did you refrain from eye contact, use particular forms of address, select particular vocabulary, or conduct the transaction orally rather than through print? In other words, how was your literate practice changed?

Increasing technological change means that new workplaces have evolved. Older economies and societies designed around 'a world of male full employment and stable nuclear families' (Leadbeater, 2000, p. 11) no longer exist, and new organisations are made up of and deal with an increasingly diverse range of social, cultural, and ethnic groups. As a result of technological change in some parts of the world, the economies of countries are becoming more about knowledge creation and service industries than about the production of crops and manufacturing industry. Many of the multinational knowledge creation and service companies are global, with employees all over the world. Leadbeater suggests that more creative and collaborative institutions are needed to deal with the 'knowledge-creating societies' (p. 11).

Call centres with centralised computer systems that deal with services such as electricity, gas, insurance, and telephone accounts are an example of companies that have evolved from technological change. These call centres may not be located in the country that is being serviced. For example, in India global call centres are growing. Consider the literacies required of someone working in such a call centre. Training for these people includes information about the culture, idioms, and interests of the countries that these call centres service to ensure the workers are able to understand and meet client needs. In addition, these workers must have knowledge of the product they are selling or servicing and the computer technology they are using.

Another example of technological change influencing workplaces is the growth of small businesses that have evolved from technology such as iPods. Some businesses offer iPod accessories so that people can have individualised-looking iPods; some will load CDs onto iPod for a fee; and other businesses are developing speakers that can be used to make iPods into home sound systems as well as portable personal ones. Consider the literacy skills of the people involved in these small businesses. They are not confined to technological literacy but involve marketing, identifying social trends, using business knowledge, and so forth. Not all these people will have all these literacies, so they will need to know how to access other literacies.

REFLECTION
STRATEGY

To increase your understanding about the phenomena we have just discussed and find examples relevant to your social and cultural context, use newspapers, television, or other media to look for stories that tell of new businesses that have evolved from technology.

1. What skills, knowledge, or ways of behaving and communicating will be required in these new businesses?

2. How might they be similar to or different from those required in a previous business?

Technology also has influenced social behaviour and therefore literate practices such as talking, listening, viewing, reading, and writing. For example, consider how etiquette for using mobile phones in public places has evolved and how it is enforced. Mobile phones have even influenced marketing and advertising techniques. Advertisers will now plant employees on public transport to talk loudly on mobile phones about a new product in order to make the product seem trendy and desirable. This technique is clearly a response to the new social behaviours that sociologists have identified amongst young mobile phone users. Such behaviours include socialising simultaneously with people physically nearby and those present via the mobile phone, as well as swarming. *Swarming* refers to the effect of using a mobile phone to contact people about a desirable place to gather. Because mobile phones can be used to contact large numbers of people quickly and easily, the effect can be a swarm of people arriving in a place all at once. This can lead to various behaviours, such as simply hanging out, gate-crashing a party, or vandalism. But the initial swarming results from literate practices with mobile phones.

REFLECTION STRATEGY

Think about how your social and literate practices have changed as a result of technology.

1. How do you keep in contact with friends and family, or conduct your financial business such as banking?
2. How did you do these things 2, 5, or 10 years ago?
3. What did you need to learn or know in order to operate in these new ways?

Technology has also led to changes in recording, sharing, and studying social and cultural events. Previously, letters and diaries were a source of social and cultural history. But now that technology allows the use of video, photos, and sound, the writing of letters and diaries has decreased and these forms are being lost. How many people keep e-mails, text messages, and so forth? In fact, some people now send seasonal greetings such as Christmas messages by a text message rather than cards. Handwriting on paper is becoming less common, and the concept of writing now includes sending text messages, photos, or video clips via e-mail, phone, or handheld devices. Students must also be able to cope with the speed with which technology makes things happen—information delivered in seconds sometimes requires immediate action.

The far-reaching technological changes of the times mean that in students' public and private lives they will encounter changing social behaviours and workplaces and must interact with different social and cultural groups on a daily basis. These interactions will occur not only face to face but also through the Internet, e-mail, and other technologies (e.g., film and media) that are now an everyday part of our workplaces, homes, and leisure activities. Students must master not only the technology but also the associated literacy practices required by the inclusion of still and moving images, sound effects, and music. In the future, students will also need communication and social skills for interacting with different groups and cultures in a variety of settings from home to workplace.

THEORY INTO PRACTICE: CLASSROOM APPLICATION

Students use technology constantly but are perhaps not aware of the ways in which technology shapes their literate practices. Therefore, they may not use technology as effectively as they might. The more conscious students are of how they go about literate practices, the more strategic and effective they will be. One way to get students to reflect on how technology shapes their literate practices is to compare similar tasks using different technologies. The purpose of the following activities is to make students more conscious of how they conduct literate practices and how technology and sociocultural factors influence literate behaviours.

Activity 1
Help students investigate the difference between shopping online for groceries and shopping at the local supermarket by having them actually take a shopping trip and then explore the online alternative. Modify the shopping task according to the interests and experiences of your students. For example, use a toy site or a Barbie or Star Wars online shopping site for younger children. Investigate the difference between going to the local gym in person and signing up for a class or a community activity such as a sport team and doing the same task by phone.

1. Before students explore each task, ask them to predict what they will do.

2. Ask students how they will cope if they are unsure about something (i.e., how they would get clarification or assistance).

3. Instruct students to compare the modes they used during each task (i.e., how much talking, listening, reading, writing, and viewing they did). Which modes were dominant in each situation and why?

4. How did the technology change the way they went about each task (e.g., face to face or by phone or Internet)?

5. Ask students if they needed to be better at particular aspects of literacy in each situation (e.g., 'Did you have to have better listening skills or prediction skills in one situation rather than another?').

Activity 2

Although students may not live in a context that has a range of social, cultural, religious, or ethnic groups, they may well encounter different groups in their adult life either face to face or through technology. Even if they are living in multicultural areas, they still may not be aware of how their literate practices may need to change when they interact with different groups. Once again, comparing real-life situations and identifying how literate practices change is a way to increase awareness.

1. Ask the students to role-play talking to an adult from a social, cultural, ethnic, or religious group different from the student's own (such as someone who does not speak the same language) and explain how to get to their school. Then role-play the same task with an adult of their own social, cultural, ethnic, or religious group.

2. Conduct an analysis similar to that in steps 2–5 in Activity 1. Discuss how the explanations would differ if students were explaining directions to someone their own age. Students also could role-play this and compare.

3. Ask students to do the same role-plays via the phone rather than face to face. Consider how the technology and the background of the person to whom they were explaining the route changed their literate practices.

Activity 3

Ask the students to explain to you and then to each other how to play one of their DVD or video games such as you might find on XBox. Ask the students to identify the games they use at home and use these for the activity. This activity will work better if you can have the game on a computer as part of the demonstration and explanation.

1. Talk about the difference between simply *playing* the game and *explaining how to play* the game.

2. Discuss how much shared knowledge and vocabulary was necessary, particularly when explaining to the adult or less experienced players.

3. Discuss the problem-solving strategies that are used when playing a new or unfamiliar game, in other words, how you work out what to do.

Technological Change and Identity

We have discussed how technology influences literate practices in workplaces and leisure, social, and civic activities, and how it shapes behaviour. However, another influence of technology is how it shapes values, beliefs, and personal identity. Through advances in, and wider availability of, technology, the purposes of technology have converged. Previously, technology was either for communicating or providing information. Now one piece of technology can fulfil both purposes; it can be a tool for communication and a tool for acquiring information. For example, digital television sets have the capability to broadcast free-to-air or pay television; provide access to the Internet; and provide a platform for computer games, CD-ROMs, DVDs, video, or satellite television. Not only do students have a broader range of knowledge and information coming to them via electronic equipment such as the television; they also have to engage in a range of social and literate behaviours in order to use the information. Students may be able to view multiple screens or pages or link to interactive elements where they chat with people all over the world, make purchases, or download personal selections of movies or music. They may need to read, print, or view moving or still images, and listen to speech, music, or sound effects simultaneously.

Consequently, the students' sense of self, or personal identity, is open to influences from, and interactions with, many different groups that hold a range of beliefs, value systems, and attitudes. As the New London Group (1996) suggests, the concept of one largely shared set of community values and conventions disseminated by the print and electronic media has been challenged by the availability of multichannel media systems and growth in the variety of print media. Such systems cater to different audiences, rather than one large homogenous audience, as more subcultures and specialist groups become a viable and important part of the market share to be courted and serviced. Servicing individualised markets, often referred to as niche marketing, has become a trend of the 21st century. Niche marketing is aided by the availability of personal computers, mobile phones, digital cameras, and video camcorders, and the ease of placing material on personal websites on the Internet. Marketing is not just the province of big business and multinational companies anymore.

There are numerous examples of niche marketing aided by the Internet across all sectors of the community. They include socially acceptable and illegal areas, from mail-order sites for organic food, specialised plants, and recipes, to sites selling pornography and instructions for bomb making. There are also membership sites for groups such as collectors, genealogy researchers, and political associations. Viewers of or participants in using these sites are exposed to the values and attitudes of group leaders who set up the sites, and a visitor's identity is potentially influenced or shaped by those attitudes or values.

Seemingly innocent sites such as Barbie.com are promulgating particular values about consumerism and a woman's role, size, shape, and behaviour in society. Consider, for example, the use of pink as the dominant colour on Barbie sites. It reinforces the stereotype of pink being a colour exclusive to girls.

It is essential for students to develop literate practices that enable them to investigate the authority of such sites and to critically examine the ideas, information, values, and attitudes presented. The maxim *you are what you eat* traditionally referred to food consumption, but it also applies to the commodities people buy and the ideas, knowledge, values, and attitudes they potentially consume via multimedia technology. Of course the food and commodities people consume are often influenced by the multimedia technology they also consume.

Globally integrated mass-marketing is aided by advances in technology. Children are typically targeted, as they tend to be frequent users of electronic media (A. Luke, 1995). The most obvious example of global integrated mass-marketing occurs with the release of movies for children. The release of the movie *Shrek* (Adamson & Jenson, 2001) was accompanied by the integrated mass-marketing of books, games, toys, food items, pencil cases, and clothes. These items were produced and sold globally as the movie was released in each country. The *Spider-Man* (Raimi, 2002), *Toy Story 2* (Lasseter, 1999), and *Monsters, Inc.* (Anderson & Doctor, 2001) movies have also been commoditised and marketed globally.

Because of their availability and ease of access, the purchase or acquisition of products, information, ideas, and values can become commonplace and regarded as part of everyday life. A consequence of uncritical consumption is that identities, values, and beliefs might be shaped unconsciously. It therefore becomes important that students' literate practices, knowledge, and skills include the ability to check the sources and authenticity of information. As critical consumers, students should be able to make informed decisions about the products they consume, thereby accepting or rejecting the knowledge, ideas, beliefs, and values attached to them.

REFLECTION
STRATEGY

The purpose of this reflection strategy is to critically examine marketing in the media and assess its potential influence on values, beliefs, and identity.

1. Compare and contrast a range of advertisements from print and electronic media. Use advertisements for different products and that target different age groups or social and cultural groups. Choose paper advertisements from magazines and newspapers, Internet advertisements, and radio and

television advertisements. Use the following questions to consider what your analyses tell you about the influence of media and marketing on values and attitudes.

- Who do you think is the targeted consumer of this product and what is it about the ad that leads you to this conclusion?
- What modes are used in the ad (e.g., printed word, music sound effects, still images, moving images)?
- How is each mode used to convey the product and make it attractive to the targeted consumer?
- Do you feel included or excluded from the targeted consumer group? What is it about the ad that makes you feel this way?

2. Conduct a similar analysis using advertisements for the same or similar products that target different cultural, economic, or social groups.

THEORY INTO PRACTICE: CLASSROOM APPLICATION

Analysing and comparing aspects of popular culture with your students, as in the Reflection Strategy above, is a useful way to get students to reflect on and articulate what attracts and influences them, potentially shaping their values, attitudes, beliefs, and identities. This activity can be completed with any age group, provided you ask the students to select the texts. Then they will have the necessary knowledge of the text, or subject, to engage in the discussion.

1. Ask the students to identify their favourite websites, movies, books, and magazines, and then use these texts as the basis for analysis and discussion.
2. Ask the students to work in groups and identify the things they like to do; types of music, books, magazines, and movies they enjoy; and their leisure activities. Compare the lists and use the information to compile a descriptor of the interests of a typical person of their age in their community. Because people of their age in the community have a variety of interests, it may be necessary to create a descriptor of more than one 'typical' student. (Do this as a whole-class activity with teacher as scribe for younger students.)
3. In the same groups, ask the students to identify the characteristics of what they believe to be a cool person in their age group and communi-

ty. Compare the lists and compile a descriptor of this cool person. This can be done with words and images.

4. Examine some of the favourite websites, movies, books, television shows, and so forth that the students identified, and discuss the following questions:

   ▸▸ Who do you think is the targeted audience of this product?

   ▸▸ What is it about the website, movie, book, or television show that leads you to this conclusion?

   ▸▸ How similar is this audience to the profile of the typical student previously identified in your group work?

   ▸▸ Do you, or would you, dress like, use the language of, or behave like any of the people in this website, movie, book, or television show?

   ▸▸ How influential do you feel this website, movie, book, or television show has been in your life?

   ▸▸ Consider whether these influences are positive or negative, and why.

   ▸▸ Did you realise the nature of the influence before we did these analyses?

5. Finish with a general discussion about how students might become more aware of and monitor the influence of popular culture on their lives in terms of its positive and negative effects.

Summary: Implications of Change for Literacy and Literacy Education

This chapter has explored change as the new constant, and the impact of globalisation and technology on social behaviours and literate practices. The trend that emerges is that literacy and literate practices encompass a greater range of knowledge, skills, processes, and behaviours than before and that these practices will continue to change. The concept of literacy as reading, writing, listening, and speaking is no longer a concept only about printed words on paper and oracy but also includes digital technology, sound, music, words, and still and moving images. The texts that students produce, or write, and consume, or read, often require processing several modes simultaneously in order to make meaning. For example, students read words, watch moving images, and listen to spoken language simultaneously when viewing a news broadcast on television. Furthermore, depending on the purpose, the context students find themselves in, and the people they are interacting with, their literate practices also include certain types of behaviour, turn taking, and role-playing. At the most rudimentary level, this means it is not sufficient simply to know the vocabulary; students need to know how and when to use it and with whom. At more sophisticated levels, it means having the problem-solving skills, flexibility, and strategic awareness to work in groups, move between tasks and workplaces, and use or adapt knowledge to live life as an active and informed citizen.

Consequently, the implications of change as the new constant for literacy education are vast and apply not only to the content of literacy programs but also to the pedagogy. Clearly, past concepts about what constitutes a text have been challenged. Being literate can no longer be regarded as being only about the printed word on paper and oracy. Literacy programs must include the ability to consume and produce the multimodal texts that are an increasingly large part of students' lives. This means being literate with still and moving images, music and sound, as well as the printed and oral word, and being able to combine them meaningfully when consuming or producing texts. This has very clear ramifications for the content of literacy programs and the links with other discipline areas such as music, art, graphics, and media studies.

However, students must not only consume and produce texts but engage in literate practices using texts in a variety of situations that require different behaviours and interactions with increasingly diverse social and cultural groups. Increasingly, they will need to work collaboratively with others towards common goals. Therefore, literacy pedagogy must teach students to be flexible, tolerant of different viewpoints, and able to problem solve, analyse situations, and work strategically. They must be able to identify the knowledge and resources they have and combine and recombine them to suit the particular purpose and context. Consequently, school classrooms and teachers' pedagogy must encourage, model, and reflect these sorts of behaviours. The content and pedagogy of literacy programs must reflect the literate practices of local to global communities and equip students for change. Educators cannot hope to teach students all they need to know, as this will change constantly. But teachers can equip their students with the knowledge, skills, strategies, and attitudes that will enable them to meet new situations and cope with them. The concept of multiliteracies was developed in response to the challenges of literacy education in a climate of constant change, which is the focus of chapter 2.

Defining Multiliteracies

I n chapter 1, we explored the increasing complexity of what constitutes literacy and literate practices in a constantly changing, socially and culturally diverse, globalised, and technological world. This chapter explores the term *multiliteracies*, a concept that has evolved in response to concern about how literacy teaching can equip students for the changing world in which they live. With that goal in mind, teachers will need to help students develop the capacity to produce, read, and interpret spoken language, print, and multimedia texts. Likewise, students will need to acquire the skills, strategies, and practices they need for work and leisure; active citizenship; participation in social, cultural, and community activities; and personal growth.

Given the impact of change on literacy and literate practices, it is appropriate at this point to consider a definition of literacy that is cognisant of these changes and supports the development of literacy programs and pedagogy. Although many people have written about these issues and their impact on literacy (e.g., Anstey, 2002a, 2002b; Freebody & Luke, 1990, 2003; Kress, 2003; Kress & van Leeuwen, 2001; Lankshear, 1997; A. Luke, 1995, 2001; Muspratt, Luke, & Freebody, 1997), A. Luke and Freebody (2000) provide one of the more recent and useful definitions of literacy: 'Literacy is the flexible and sustainable mastery of a repertoire of practices with the texts of traditional and new communications technologies via spoken, print, and multimedia' (p. 9). This definition provides the key to identifying the characteristics of a literate person, and those characteristics provide direction for programs and pedagogy. The definition leads to the conclusion that a literate person

➤➤ is *flexible*—is positive and strategically responsive to changing literacies;

➤➤ is able to *sustain mastery*—knows enough to be able to reformulate current knowledge or access and learn new literate practices;

➤➤ has a *repertoire of practices*—has a range of knowledge, skills, and strategies to use when appropriate;

➤➤ is able to *use traditional texts*—uses print and paper, and face-to-face oral encounters; and

➤➤ is able to *use new communications technologies*—uses digital and electronic texts that have multiple modes (e.g., spoken and written), often simultaneously.

Although this definition provides direction, it does not incorporate concepts about the social context of literacy, that is, the literate practices of our changing world. On its own this definition does not address what a literate person needs to know and be able to do to operate successfully in the contexts in which literacy is used. These contexts would include using literacy for work and leisure; active citizenship; participation in social, cultural, and community activities; and personal growth. The concept of multiliteracies attempts to address both the defining of literacy and the implications of the practices needed for the many and varied contexts of a 21st-century life.

Origin of the Term *Multiliteracies*

In 1994 a group of international literacy educators met in New London, New Hampshire, USA, to consider how literacy teaching should respond to the rapid change being wrought by increasing globalisation, technology, and social diversity (Cope & Kalantzis, 2000). Their discussions began by focussing on the desirable social outcomes of being literate and the pedagogies necessary to achieve them. The result of their discussions was the term *multiliteracies* and a paper entitled 'A Pedagogy of Multiliteracies: Designing Social Futures' (New London Group, 1996). Although much has been written about multiliteracies since this original article, the origins of the term and in particular the title of the article are important to understanding the concept. The title emphasises the notion that fostering multiliteracies is as much about pedagogy as it is about literacy, and that the focus of educational endeavours is to prepare students for social futures in which they actively participate and influence; that is, they are the designers of their social futures.

Unpacking the Term *Multiliteracies*

The *multi* in multiliteracies can be thought of in a number of ways. Broadly, it refers to the range of literacies and literate practices used in all sectors of life and how these literate practices are similar and different. For example, the literate practices used in the supermarket when selecting and purchasing groceries differ from those used in leisure activities such as interacting with friends in a sporting team or club. Some ways they are different include which modes are used most (oral or written), the specialised vocabulary, the formality or informality of address between participants, and what is considered acceptable spelling, grammar, punctuation, or intonation in the situation.

There are two major categories that encompass the range of multiple literacies. With the growth of technology, a person must be literate not only with paper text but also with live (e.g., face-to-face) encounters and electronic works. This means being literate in multiple modes. For this reason, the term *text* throughout this book encompasses the subject or content of a work or activity in written, electronic, or live forms. The second category is the context in which literacy is practiced. Students need to able to use appropriate literate practices in many different contexts. That is, to be multiliterate, a student must first recognise that a context requires different literate practices and then be able to modify known literate practices or use them in new and different ways. The *multi* in multiliteracies is about the necessity to have multiple forms of knowledge and understandings about literacy and social contexts that enable appropriate and successful performance in all aspects of life.

These concepts about the relationship between literacy and context are not altogether new. In the 1960s and 1970s, concern about the differences between students' language ability led researchers to examine students' social and cultural backgrounds and how they influenced language learning. Labov (1969) developed the concept of *linguistic relativity*, suggesting that a child's language development was influenced by the social and cultural context in which he or she grew up. The concept of linguistic relativity was considered an explanation for difference—that is, social and cultural background defined language ability. Cazden (1967, 1972) took these ideas further and suggested that although linguistic relativity accounted for a person's initial knowledge of language, he or she could develop the ability and knowledge necessary to move between contexts and use the appropriate language. Cazden referred to this as *communicative competence*. More recently, Gee (1992, 1996) discussed similar concepts, extending these ideas to the development of a range of literacies and literate practices (discourses and Discourses) and examined the ways in which literacy pedagogy can assist in this development. Lowercase *discourses* refers to listening, speaking, reading, and writing, or literacies. *Discourses* with a capital *D* refers to all of the attitudes and behaviours associated with the use of those different literacies. It is no surprise that Cazden and Gee discuss important components of the term *multiliteracies*—flexibility; multiple forms of knowledge; and the relationships between literate practices, contexts, and social, cultural, and behavioural aspects of literacy—because they were part of the New London Group and those early multiliteracies discussions.

REFLECTION
STRATEGY

The purpose of this reflection strategy is to identify the multiple literacies and literate practices in different contexts of your life. Use these reflections to develop understandings about both the literacy and socio-cultural dimensions of multiliteracies, develop an appreciation of the complexity of being literate in a variety of contexts, and further develop understandings that literacy is about both cognition (i.e., thinking) and behaviour.

1. Identify three different contexts in which you have recently practiced literacy. Try to make sure they involve different groups of people and different types and modes of text (for example, a work situation such as conducting a meeting, a leisure situation such as playing a game or going to the movies and coffee with friends, and a civic situation such as looking up the local council website to find out about dog registration).

2. Complete the following retrieval chart as a way of identifying the multiple literacies you use across these situations. The first column has been completed as an example.

	Task 1: Making a Doctor's Appointment	Task 2:	Task 3:
Context	Home		
Modes (oral, written)	Oral, written		
Type of texts (electronic, paper, or live)	Electronic, paper		
Characteristics of texts or genre	Phone book, set out alphabetically in a list		
Relationship with participants (equal or unequal, formal or informal, your position in the hierarchy of the context)	Formal, unequal		
Relative formality of grammar, spelling, punctuation, specialised language	Oral: precise, specialised language (e.g., time, medical terms) Written: informal (notation for appointment book is for personal use only)		
Types of visual text used (e.g., charts, moving images, tables, graphs, photos, etc.)	Appointment book with graphic display Phone book with alphabetised list		
Types of oral text used (e.g., music, voice, sound effects, etc.)	Voice to make telephone inquiry, sound effects indicating the number I dialled was engaged, music I listened to when phone was put on hold.		

3. Think about what you needed to know and be able to do in order to complete each task successfully:

- Compare the special literacy knowledge required in each context. What was similar or different? Which modes were dominant in each?

- Compare the different social contexts and think about the similar and different social knowledge you needed in order to perform appropriately and successfully.

- Think about how, where, and when you learned what you needed to know to operate successfully in these contexts.

In each situation, you probably engaged in multiple modes and behaved differently. The knowledge you needed was specialised literacy knowledge and social and cultural knowledge—that is, special knowledge about the context and participants. You did not learn all this when you were young or at school. You learned in different aspects of your life as it became necessary. Being multiliterate means having the capacity to continue to modify or add to one's knowledge about literacy and literate practices.

- -

Multiliteracies means being cognitively and socially literate with paper, live, and electronic texts. It also means being strategic, that is, being able to recognise what is required in a given context, examine what is already known, and then, if necessary, modify that knowledge to develop a strategy that suits the context and situation. A multiliterate person must therefore be a problem solver and strategic thinker, that is, an active and informed citizen.

Because of the advances in technology and the many contexts in which we now operate, we are often exposed to or are required to access large amounts of information from many and varied sources. We must be aware that the texts we access or are exposed to have been consciously constructed to share particular information in particular ways, shaping our attitudes, values, and behaviours. Some information might be omitted and some might be overemphasised or presented in an attractive manner, using sound, colour, or layout in manipulative ways. Therefore, being multiliterate must also involve being critically literate, that is, having the ability to analyse texts, identify their origins and authenticity, and understand how they have been constructed in order to perceive their gaps, silences, and biases.

In summary, multiliteracies focus on how literacy and literate practices have been influenced by local and global, social, cultural, and technological change. They focus on

> ⇥ technology and the increase of multimedia (texts constructed using different media such as newspaper or television) and multimodal texts (those that draw on different modes, such as listening and speaking) and

> ⇥ the influence of increasing social, cultural, and linguistic diversity on literacy, literate practices, and critical literacy.

Anstey (2002b) defines a multiliterate person as flexible and strategic and able to understand and use literacy and literate practices

> ⇥ with a range of texts and technologies;

> ⇥ in socially responsible ways;

> ⇥ in a socially, culturally, and linguistically diverse world; and

> ⇥ to fully participate in life as an active and informed citizen.

Implications for Pedagogy

A pedagogy for multiliteracies must focus on the major areas in which technological and socio-cultural changes have had an impact on everyday life. The most obvious of these is the changing nature of texts that has arisen from advances in technology. A multiliterate person must have understandings about text that include the impact of social, cultural, and technological change. However, there are two other areas that are equally important. The first of these other two areas is the concept of literacy as social practice. A multiliterate person must be aware of his or her social and literate practices, or literacy identity, in order to be strategic and flexible in a changing world. The final area of impact for pedagogy is the area of critical literacy. A multiliterate person must be able to critically analyse texts and contexts and take informed action.

Understandings About Text

The following understandings about text are distilled from the body of work on multiliteracies and social–cultural views of literacy (e.g., Cope & Kalantzis, 1997, 2003; Durrant & Green, 2000; Freebody & Luke, 2003; Hagood, 2000; Unsworth, 2002; Zammit & Downes, 2002).

> ⇥ A text may be paper, electronic, or live.

> ⇥ A text may comprise one or more semiotic systems.

> ⇥ Texts are consciously constructed.

> ⇥ Meanings are actively constructed.

> ⇥ A text may have several possible meanings.

» A text may be constructed using intertextuality.

» Texts may be multimodal, interactive, linear, and nonlinear.

A literacy program that is focussed on developing multiliteracies would use each of these understandings as an outcome. In order to plan a program, the knowledge and strategies needed to meet the outcome should be identified, and particular pedagogies will need to be selected (see chapter 3).

Paper, Electronic, or Live Texts

If multiliteracies focus on technology and the emergence of multimedia texts, and a multiliterate person must be literate with a range of texts and technologies, then one of the implications for pedagogy is to examine the definition of text in a multimedia age. A text conveys meaning to a group of people. It is delivered by a platform and may comprise one or more modes. The platform by which it is delivered may be electronic (for example a mobile phone or computer), live (person to person or a live performance such as a play), or paper (such as a newspaper or book). Live texts include music, drama or art. Having identified the texts students need to become familiar with, it is necessary to identify what students need to know and be able to do with those texts.

Semiotic Systems

Students make meaning of a text by understanding and interpreting the text's sets of signs or symbols, which are called semiotic systems. There are five semiotic systems:

1. linguistic (oral and written language, for example, use vocabulary and grammar),

2. visual (still and moving images, for example, use colour, vectors, and viewpoint),

3. auditory (music and sound effects, for example, use volume, pitch, and rhythm),

4. gestural (facial expression and body language, for example, use movement speed and stillness), and

5. spatial (layout and organisation of objects and space, for example, use proximity, direction, and position).

For example, linguistic semiotic systems include letters, words, sentences, and paragraphs. One of the conventions of the linguistic semiotic system is the set of grammar rules that organise the words, phrases, and sentences so a reader can make meaning of them. Similarly, the conventions of punctuation help the reader make meaning of the linguistic semiotic system.

Previously, the linguistic semiotic system dominated literacy pedagogy because texts mainly comprised oral or written language. However, because texts are increasingly multimodal, a literate person must have mastery of all five semiotic systems and understand how they work together in a text to convey meaning. This has significant implications for selecting content and balancing a literacy program. The issue of teaching students about the consumption and production of texts comprising multiple semiotic systems is addressed in more detail in chapter 5.

REFLECTION
STRATEGY

The purpose of this reflection strategy is to focus on the range of semiotic systems that you use, how the semiotic systems work together to convey meaning, and how purpose and context affect the selections and use of semiotic systems.

1. Identify a live, an electronic, and a paper text you have used recently.

2. Analyse each text using the retrieval chart below to identify which semiotic systems are used in them and how they are used. The analyses for a live text have been filled in as an example.

Text Details	Linguistic Semiotic System	Gestural Semiotic System	Auditory Semiotic System	Spatial Semiotic System	Visual Semiotic System
Identify the purpose of the text and context in which it is used.	How is it used and what meanings are conveyed through it?	How is it used, and what meanings are conveyed through it?	How is it used, and what meanings are conveyed through it?	How is it used, and what meanings are conveyed through it?	How is it used, and what meanings are conveyed through it?
Paper Text:					
Electronic Text:					
Live Text: Used by a mime artist to entertain passers-by as part of street theatre	Not used	Gesture is used to convey emotion (sadness and isolation) through body position (slumped) and facial expression (mouth turned down and eyes downcast)	Not used	Positioned away from other people, leaving large amount of space, turned back to others to depict isolation and sadness	Not used

3. Examine the chart you have completed and think about

   - which texts used which semiotic systems,

   - the relationship between the purpose and the semiotic systems used,

   - the relationship between the context and the semiotic systems used, and

   - whether the efficacy of the text might have been improved if the selection and use of the semiotic systems had been different.

THEORY INTO PRACTICE: CLASSROOM APPLICATION

It is important to raise students' awareness of the variety of semiotic systems employed in texts and help them recognise that texts may be paper, electronic, and live. Use discussions to help students become more strategic about how they approach tasks with texts and to think about the text more carefully so that they know what knowledge they will need to access. Discussions should also focus students on the purpose and context of the task to ensure that they think about the strategies they will need to employ to get the task done.

1. Discuss the characteristics of text as a routine part of using texts in the classroom. Points for discussion should include attention to the

   ▸▸ type of text being used (paper, electronic, or live);

   ▸▸ purpose of the text and context in which it is being used;

   ▸▸ semiotic systems employed;

   ▸▸ types of information conveyed by each semiotic system;

   ▸▸ identification of relationships between the semiotic systems used, the type of text, purpose, and context; and

   ▸▸ critical analysis of the semiotic systems used and their effectiveness for this purpose and context.

   These discussions can occur in groups, as a whole class, or as individual investigations to be shared.

2. Use a retrieval chart (such as the one in the Reflection Strategy on page 26) as the focus of a whole-group discussion. It is an effective way of collecting and analysing data about the text because students can see the data and think about the relationships.

3. Review well-constructed and poorly constructed texts. If critical analysis reveals flaws or shortcomings, reconstruct the text to make it more effective, using a different type of text (paper, electronic, or live) and different combinations of semiotic systems.

Consciously Constructed Texts

No text is neutral. All texts are constructed for a particular purpose—for example, entertainment, procedural, economic, or political reasons. Furthermore, they are constructed in a particular way to suit that purpose. Depending on the context in which they will be used, the intended audience, and the platforms of delivery available, texts will comprise a particular set of semiotic systems. Particular structures (genres) will have been selected that suit the purpose, context, audience, platform, and semiotic systems.

Competent consumers and producers of text understand about the conscious construction of a text. As consumers of text, students can use signals—such as the structure or genre and the way in which semiotic systems have been used—to identify the purpose of the text and how it should be used. As producers of text, they can use the same knowledge and understandings to construct and shape texts that achieve their purposes.

An important concept related to understandings about the conscious construction of text is author's intent. This concept suggests that the author constructed the text with the intent of persuading the reader in some way, for example, to understand a particular point of view or that an event occurred in a particular way. Author intent, although still relevant, now has to be considered in a number of ways. For example, many texts—particularly those that are multimodal—are constructed or authored by several people. These might be the author of the words; the photographer or artist who supplied the illustrations; the editor who wrote the brief for the author and the photographer or artist, and edited the written copy; the designer who organised the layout and selected fonts, colour, and style; and the marketing manager who set a budget which constrained any or all of these decisions.

Actively Constructed Meanings

Although producers of texts consciously construct them and attempt to shape consumers' meaning making, it is the consumer of the text that actively constructs the meaning. The consumer brings all his or her social, cultural, and literate knowledge to the text, which will influence the way the consumer makes meaning of the text. The context in which the consumer uses the text will also influence the meanings made.

REFLECTION
STRATEGY

The purpose of this reflection strategy is to explore personal experiences in which you have actively constructed meaning and the influences upon your meaning making.

1. Have you ever viewed a movie a second time in a different context, perhaps a decade after seeing it the first time, or with different people, or maybe after things in your life have changed quite a bit? Think of a text—such as a film, television program, book, or poem—that over time has changed for you. Try to identify why it has changed.

2. Have you ever been to a movie with friends and when discussing it afterwards found that you had quite different perceptions about its focus or meaning? Think about why that was the case. Probably it was because each of you had different resources, knowledge, beliefs, or attitudes that influenced your construction of meaning.

3. Next time this happens explore with your friends what it was that influenced your meaning making.

- -

THEORY INTO PRACTICE: CLASSROOM APPLICATION

Consider how the backgrounds of your students might be influencing their meaning making. Sometimes their lack of comprehension may stem from a lack of general, social, or cultural knowledge and experience rather than a lack of literacy knowledge or ability. When you are introducing a new literacy skill ensure that the text you choose does not get in the way of students' learning. For example, using a text about the sea for literate practices that require knowledge of what it feels like to swim in waves and be tossed around may not be useful for students without experience of the sea. The following steps and questions might aid in the selection of texts:

1. What is the purpose of using the text? For example, is it the vehicle through which students will learn, practice, or revise a new literacy skill; engage in recreational reading; or learn content in another subject area?

2. Consider whether the text will be read independently or with the assistance of an adult reader.

3. Think about how familiar the content, vocabulary, text type (i.e., live, written, or electronic), and structure need to be, and then use that information to select the text.

Several Possible Meanings

As discussed previously, the consumers of the text actually make the particular meaning that is significant to them, despite the producers' attempts to shape the text to emphasise a specific meaning. In the reflection strategy on pages 28–29, we explored how and why meanings might change, that is, a consumer might perceive different meanings at different times or in different contexts or if using the text for a different purpose. Therefore, texts can have several possible meanings to different consumers or to the same consumer at different times. This does not mean that any meaning is correct; clearly one has to be able to justify one's meaning.

It is also possible that a text may be deliberately constructed with several possible meanings. For example, postmodern picture books are often constructed to have more than one meaning, so children of all ages can enjoy them. There will be ideas, concepts, and aspects of the illustrations that appeal to different age groups (see chapter 4 for more on this subject). The makers of children's movies increasingly provide a range of possible meanings to ensure that adults are as entertained as children, which increases ticket sales. A good example of this is the movie *Shrek* (Adamson & Jenson, 2001), which has ideas and humour that rely on adult prior knowledge about marketing and competition between moviemakers, as well as humour and a plot suitable for children.

The concept that texts may have several possible meanings is an important one for students to grasp as consumers and producers of text. If as consumers of text they are aware of the factors that produce multiple meanings (e.g., prior knowledge, social and cultural experience, the way a text is constructed, the choice of words or illustrations), then they will have more control and expertise when constructing and producing a text themselves. They will be aware of the factors that would need to be controlled tightly when constructing a text, such as safety notices or instructions that must be interpreted exactly. Similarly, when engaged in an oral text with other participants, students can use their awareness to avoid ambiguities or offence that might arise from certain constructions and selection of vocabulary.

Intertextuality

One of the techniques producers use to construct text is intertextuality, which refers to the ways one text might draw on or resemble the characteristics of another, causing the consumer of the text to make links between them. There are a number of ways this might happen:

> ►► A text might parody the generic structure of another—for example, a biographical article might be written in the style of a fairy tale in order to emphasise the person's good fortune or rags-to-riches life story.

> ►► The layout of a text might mimic the layout of another type of text—for example a page in a book might be set out to resemble a website so that it appeals to a younger audience.

- A scene in a movie might draw on a scene from another movie—for example, in *Titanic* (Cameron, 1997) there was a memorable scene in which the main female character stands at the bow of the ship, arms flung out and leaning into the wind. A similar scene is often seen in other movies when characters are sailing or in boats of some kind. Phrases or music are also often used across movies.
- A pastiche of genres, artistic media, and styles might be used in making a hybrid text that requires intertextual knowledge to make sense of the text. For example, some postmodern picture books such as *Tagged* (Crew, 1997) combine illustrations, photographic material, and comic strips in one text. Another example of a text that draws on many genres and styles is the nonfiction science text *This Book Really Sucks!* (Planet Dexter, 1999), which examines the scientific phenomena of suction and gravity.

When a producer consciously manipulates a text in this way, he or she is assuming that the consumer has the knowledge and experience to make the intertextual links and therefore the meaning intended by the producer. However, this may not always be the case. Because the consumer will actively make meaning with the knowledge and resources he or she has available, many meanings are possible. Nevertheless, an important part of being multiliterate is understanding about intertextuality and therefore looking for and making use of the intertextual links provided. It is also important for students to think about why these intertextual links are there and how they influence meaning making.

THEORY INTO PRACTICE: CLASSROOM APPLICATION

Use *The Jolly Postman* (1986) by Janet and Allen Ahlberg with students to commence understandings about intertextuality. Used in the context of learning about intertextuality, it is a good book for any age group. Understanding the actual letters that the postman delivers and which are provided in envelopes within the book relies heavily on intertextual knowledge of fairy tales—such as Little Red Riding Hood and Goldilocks and the Three Bears—and of other genres such as junk mail, as well as on general knowledge about legal issues such as reparation for damages. Keep in mind that knowledge of these fairy tales is not always shared by all students in the class, and therefore it might not be the best book for all classes. An excellent movie to use, for similar reasons, is *Shrek* (Adamson & Jenson, 2001). If you use *Shrek*, identify and examine one scene that requires intertextual knowledge as a focus for discussions rather than trying to view the whole movie.

1. After introducing the concept and talking about it with two examples such as these, it is useful to ask students to start collecting examples of intertextuality from their lives.

2. Make an intertextuality wall on which to display print examples, and think of ways to collect and display electronic examples (perhaps on CD for display on a computer screen in the room). The following retrieval chart can be provided for students to fill in and display alongside the examples they find.

> ▶▶ Details of item found (title, publication details, context found, purpose of text): for example, *Advertisement for ___ in ___ Magazine, p. 3, June 2005.*
>
> ▶▶ Type of intertextuality (What did you need to know about?): for example, *Scene and costume from the movie ___ .*
>
> ▶▶ How the intertextuality influenced or changed your meaning making (What did it emphasise or add?): for example, *It made me think more about ___ .*

3. Remember to review the wall frequently in terms of the types of intertextual links (e.g., genre, idea, scene, plot) and see if everyone was able to make those links. Students need to understand that intertextuality is related to experience and the ability to recognise, recall, and use that experience.

Multimodal, Interactive, Linear, and Nonlinear Texts

As we have stated previously, because texts are delivered by a range of platforms and may be electronic, paper, or live, they will use a variety of modes and semiotic systems. Consequently they may be engaged with in various ways. Rather than simply consuming the text, the reader or viewer may actually interact with it, for example, participating in a conversation or chat room, purchasing off the Internet, or downloading and remixing text to make a new text. While traditionally the path through a print text in English is left to right, top to bottom, and sequential, the interactive nature of electronic texts often means that rather than working through the text in this linear fashion, the consumer may choose any number of paths through the text. Even print texts now provide and encourage these options as multiple pathways and alternative endings in books that enable readers to 'choose your own adventure'. Movies are not always linear; some go from the end to the beginning (e.g., *Memento*, Nolan, 2000), and others have alternative paths and endings (e.g., *Sliding Doors*, Howitt, 1998).

A consequence of understanding these changing characteristics of text is that students need to be more strategic in the ways in which they use them.

Prior to engaging with a text they need to think about their purpose and then examine the text and how it shapes engagement. If it is a nonlinear text with many paths, then the reader needs to develop a strategy that will enable the purpose to be achieved most efficiently and effectively.

THEORY INTO PRACTICE: CLASSROOM APPLICATION

Encourage students to examine texts and select a strategy for engagement by moving students into groups at the beginning of a literacy task (for example, finding information).

1. Ask each group to identify a strategy that could be used to get the task done. (With very young students it might be best to do this with one familiar task to begin with and do it as a whole-class activity with teacher as scribe.)

2. Instruct students to analyse the task, examine the text to be used and its characteristics, and then identify a strategy. For example, if a student has to use a website to find information, the strategy might be to use the search mechanism on the site. Then the student would need to think about how to identify the appropriate words or questions to put in the search mechanism.

3. When the class comes back together, ask students to share strategies and decide which one might be the most effective; then try it and evaluate it. Whether they choose the best strategy or not is irrelevant. If it does not work, the discussion about why it did not work and the students' attempts to find a better strategy will be most instructive.

4. After sharing the strategies they have identified, each group could try out its own strategy. After trying strategies in groups, a whole-class discussion could compare the effectiveness of each strategy. The more these types of investigations and discussions become part of classroom routines, the more strategic and flexible students will become, which is an important part of being multiliterate.

Continuing Change in Texts

As technology and society continue to change, texts will continue to change. It is impossible to predict the knowledge that students will need in the future. However, it is possible to teach them basic knowledge, strategies, attitudes, and behaviours that will enable them to deal with evolving texts. Therefore, teachers must remind students that literacy and literate practices are not static. Teachers also must ensure that their pedagogy and content provide students with opportunities to be flexible and strategic problem solvers.

Literacy Identity

By examining multiliteracies and the understandings about text that a student needs in order to be multiliterate, teachers can see that literate practices are inextricably linked with social and cultural life and experiences. Because all literate practices are a reflection of the socio-cultural processes and knowledge of the learner, they are not static but dynamic and ever changing (Tusting, 2000).

Barton, Hamilton, and Ivanič (2000) state that life experiences provide everyone with a repertoire of resources about literacy and literate practices and that these experiences and resources contribute to each person's overall identity. Similar groups of related experiences form domains within a person's identity, and he or she draws on these domains in order to engage in literate practices and to make meaning. Cope and Kalantzis (2000) identify these different domains or identities collectively as discourse worlds and suggest that students draw on two in particular to make meaning, the lifeworld (i.e., everything that exists outside school) and the school-based world. Note that sometimes *lifeworld* is referred to as the real world, as though school is not part of the real world. We prefer the term *lifeworld* as this does not set up an artificial distinction. Anstey and Bull (2004) suggest that these domains or discourse worlds also help form a person's literacy identity, providing a repertoire of resources that a person can draw on when engaging in literate practices. In Figure 1, a person's literacy identity is represented as the intersection of knowledge and experience with literacy from his or her school-based world and lifeworld.

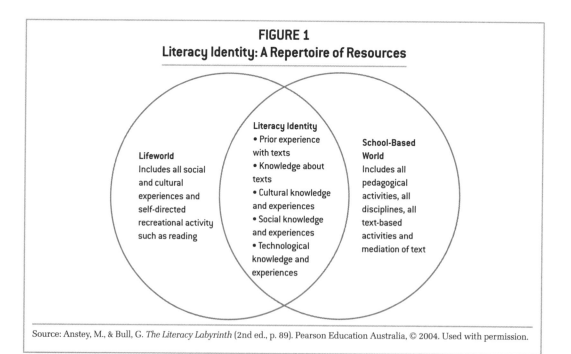

FIGURE 1
Literacy Identity: A Repertoire of Resources

Lifeworld
Includes all social and cultural experiences and self-directed recreational activity such as reading

Literacy Identity
• Prior experience with texts
• Knowledge about texts
• Cultural knowledge and experiences
• Social knowledge and experiences
• Technological knowledge and experiences

School-Based World
Includes all pedagogical activities, all disciplines, all text-based activities and mediation of text

Source: Anstey, M., & Bull, G. *The Literacy Labyrinth* (2nd ed., p. 89). Pearson Education Australia, © 2004. Used with permission.

Part of being multiliterate is being aware of one's literacy identity as a set of resources that can be used to complete a literate task. If teachers help students learn to use their literacy identities in this way they will become more flexible and strategic about literate activities. They will learn to reflect on and combine and recombine their resources to complete tasks. Note that the student's literacy identity includes social and cultural resources, technological experience, and all previous life experiences, as well as specific literacy knowledge and experience. Because literacy is a social practice, being literate goes beyond specific literacy knowledge to include social and cultural behaviour.

The concept of literacy identity is pivotal to being multiliterate. What students know, understand, and can do with texts rely on being aware of the resources available to them, that is, the knowledge and experience that make up students' literacy identities. If in reviewing those resources students find that they do not have the precise ones needed, then they can use what they have in different ways, combining and recombining resources to suit the tasks. Failing this, students can review what they do know or have that might provide avenues for seeking new information. Regardless of whether students already have the knowledge, they will need to review and remake it or go and find more. The starting point is always the person's literacy identity: the sum total of what he or she already knows and can do. Therefore, it is critical that teachers show students how to know and use their literacy identities.

One of the ways we often close down students' use of their whole literacy identity (both their lifeworld and school-based resources) comes from the socialisation of school. The socialisation of school refers to the accepted behaviour and routines of school. For example, teachers ask questions, students answer them, and teachers tell the students whether the answer is right or wrong. One of the routine questions that can close down use of the literacy identity is 'What do you know about this subject?' This question is often asked at the beginning of a lesson to get students to review previous learning. Students often hear this question as 'What have we learned at school about this subject?' The problem with hearing the question this way is that students are not drawing on all their resources to answer the real question 'What do you know about this subject?' If they are not using all the resources available, then they are not seeing the connection between school-based experiences and lifeworld experiences.

THEORY INTO PRACTICE: CLASSROOM APPLICATION

To encourage students to draw on both their school-based world and lifeworld knowledge and experience, we would suggest using discussion questions at the beginning of the lesson that are more focussed around the types of knowledge identified in the intersecting circles of Figure 1.

Following are some example questions set out under the areas identified. They are suitable for most levels of schooling, although the language may need to be modified for younger students:

Prior Experience With Texts and Knowledge About Texts

» Have you seen a text like this before?

» Where was it?

» What was it used for?

» How did you use it?

» What characteristics of that text are similar or different to this one?

» How would that affect the way we will use this text for this purpose?

» Is this a genre you have used before?

» What is this genre generally used for?

» If this text is similar in structure to the _____ genre, how might that help us use this text?

Cultural and Social Knowledge and Experience

» Have you used texts like this in similar contexts?

» How did you behave with the text in those contexts?

» Have you interacted with people before when engaging in this type of task?

» How might this previous experience help you here?

» What do you know about this social or cultural group (or context) that might help you work out the best way of going about this task?

Technological Knowledge and Experience

» Have you used this technology before?

» What do you know that might be useful in this situation?

» Are there aspects of this software/technology that are unfamiliar and you need to know more about before you can continue with this task?

A final point is that students need to be aware that their literacy identities can hinder them as well as be useful. Particular social or cultural experiences may influence how well they can complete certain tasks. For example, among some groups, religious literacy practices focus on literal recall and recitation. If these religious literacy practices are the students' main experiences with text, then they will have fewer resources to draw on when a task requires predicting or critical analysis. Similarly, a lack of technological experience might prevent students from engaging in a literacy task that they could otherwise complete. In this situation the student should review his or her resources, find that they are insufficient, and then recognise from their already acquired knowledge where to obtain further advice about the strategies that need modification.

Critical Literacy

In 1993, A. Luke suggested that students build their identities and futures in relation to the cultural texts they encounter. The ways of behaving, contexts, values, and attitudes students find in texts provide ways for them to interpret and explain the world and their place in it. The texts students encounter are often used in very powerful settings such as religious or family settings, schools, and libraries. Therefore, the messages they contain are seen as accepted or endorsed by society. Because of this, texts often contribute to the maintenance of inequity. Students now are exposed to an even greater range of texts via the Internet and other electronic forms, and the mere fact that they have been published can imply to uninformed consumers that these texts carry authority and are factual.

There are two possible responses to these ideas when selecting texts for use in the classroom. One is for the teacher to limit the texts and review their content carefully, using only texts that meet an agreed-on set of criteria regarding the topics, values, and attitudes of the content. This approach would ensure that students met only appropriate texts in school, but it would not equip them to deal with texts outside school that presented contrasting ideas, values, and attitudes, often very carefully disguised. A second response, which more appropriately supports multiliteracies goals, is for teachers to ensure that a broad range of texts are available and help students develop the skills to analyse these texts. Students will then learn how to identify a text's origins and authority and examine how the texts are attempting to shape their values and beliefs. In this way students will become more discriminatory and have skills to deal with texts they encounter in many different contexts.

Concern about the need to regard texts critically and to examine their authenticity and authority has made critical literacy a central tenet of multiliteracies. If students are not taught to take a critical perspective with texts and practice critical literacy in all contexts, then they may be marginalised, discriminated against, or unable to take an active and informed place in life. In short, the student will not be in control of his or her social future.

THEORY INTO PRACTICE: CLASSROOM APPLICATION

If students are to have critical perspectives about texts they must be taught to ask questions that aim to identify the ideologies, identities, and values that are being presented. The following questions (adapted from Anstey & Bull, 2000) might help:

1. What values or attitudes are being presented and how do they relate to my own and others'? (For younger students, ask, do these people do the sorts of things or behave the way I do?)
2. Are there contradictions in the ideologies of the text?
3. Are there gaps and silences in the text—who is represented and who is not?
4. What practices are being shaped and valued? (For younger students, ask, is this text trying to make me behave in a particular way or do things that maybe I don't want to or don't need to do?)
5. What histories and experiences are included or omitted? (For younger students, ask, are there people like me and my friends in this text?)
6. How does this text relate to my position in society and my cultural situation?

When thinking about teaching students to interrogate, or examine, texts, it is important, as teachers, to remember that the term *texts* includes paper, electronic, and live texts. In this way teachers can help students transfer critical literacy to the everyday tasks of life, from orally negotiating a timetable or permission to do something, to surfing the Internet for information for an assignment, to watching their favourite television programs. In each of these situations there will be a text that carries particular perspectives and has the capacity to affect the student in some way. Therefore, in each of these situations the student needs to be self-aware, asking questions about who is participating, what perspectives the participants have, how their involvement affects the student's position in this situation, and what the student will need to do in this situation.

It is apparent from these examples that the concept of critical literacy goes beyond simply interrogating texts; it applies to all literate practices and involves taking action. If students apply critical literacy in these ways, they will be involved not only in the communication aspects of literate practice but in *transformation*. The concept of transformation is an important one. It refers to the fact that every time students participate in literate practices they are transformed in some way as they use knowledge, skills, strategies, and ideas in new ways or in new contexts. In short, their literacy identities are transformed. By using critical literacy in all aspects of life, not only are students transformed, but they also might possibly transform or influence community, economic, or political life. This is not as idealistic as it may first sound. Many of the changes to law or changing attitudes have arisen from people taking action as a result of the critical analysis of an injustice or inequity (e.g., laws regarding racial vilification, women's rights, the right to vote, desegregation, and consumer rights). The implication for pedagogy is that when students explore critical literacy it must be with a range of texts, across all discipline areas, and in everyday situations. Teachers should also endeavour to provide opportunities for students to participate in activities in which they see and experience the impact that critical literacy can have on their own and others' lives.

REFLECTION STRATEGY

The purpose of this reflection strategy is to look at how one school applied critical literacy and achieved transformation and to think about the everyday situations in which we could and should apply critical literacy. As part of a personal development and health program, one school's leaders asked a well-known Olympic sportswoman to speak to students about training, nutrition, and motivation. The local newspaper had been invited, and representatives came and listened to the talk, took photographs, and published an article a few days later. The students had awaited the publication with some excitement; however, when they saw the article and photograph they were very disappointed. Rather than focussing on why the person was at the school and what she talked about, the article referred only to the looks of the sportswoman and her sporting and mothering achievements. Even the photograph portrayed the sportswoman in a seductive rather than businesslike way by picturing her from a bottom-up viewpoint, sitting alone on the brick fence of the school.

After critically analysing the article and photo, to ensure their first impressions were correct, the students took action. They wrote to the journalist and photographer and pointed out the way the article had positioned the sportswoman and had marginalised the reason she was at the school—to support the school's program. Interestingly, they got a reply that acknowledged that the article had done the things the students claimed and that possibly it could have dealt with the news more accurately and from a different perspective. Newspaper staff even came back to the school, found out more about the program, and published a small news item about it in a later paper. The students were thrilled to see that they could take action and achieve some measure of justice.

There are two great outcomes to this story: First, the students got to see and experience critical literacy achieve transformation. Second, they now have knowledge and skills to apply critically in other situations. An interesting aside to this story is how the photo was taken. The sportswoman allowed herself to be portrayed in the photograph in what students viewed as a seductive pose. When the photographer positioned her and took the photo from a bottom-up viewpoint, she agreed. She could have said, 'No, I think it would be more appropriate to include some of the students in the photo; after all, that is why I am here.' However her choice was to allow the photographer to construct her in this way. Whether this was a critically aware choice, we do not know.

1. Have you ever been in a similar situation in which you found yourself manipulated before you even thought about it? Think about marketing, banking, or medical situations and workplace settings.
2. What was the context?
3. How was the manipulation achieved?
4. How and why did you allow the manipulation to happen?

Achieving Balance With Multiliteracies

Teaching to foster multiliteracies requires an understanding of the characteristics of a multiliterate person, as shown in Figure 2. This description of a multiliterate person is presented as a figure so that the visual layout will shape the way the reader attends to the written text in the figure. The layout focusses first on multiliterate behaviours through the verbs *interpret*, *use*, and *produce*. Next the layout draws attention to three ways in which these behaviours would be used through the four groups of words spaced down the oval, after the group of verbs. These three groups of words emphasise texts, purpose, and context. Finally the relationships between text, purpose, and context are emphasised through the single words (prepositions) between them (*for* and *in*).

This description can help shape guidelines for balancing a multiliteracies curriculum: The curriculum should focus on the strategies and behaviours that students need, the types of texts and semiotic systems they will need to become proficient with, and the purposes and contexts they will need to learn about and experience. Despite these useful guidelines, ultimately teachers will need an answer to the question, 'What do our students need to know

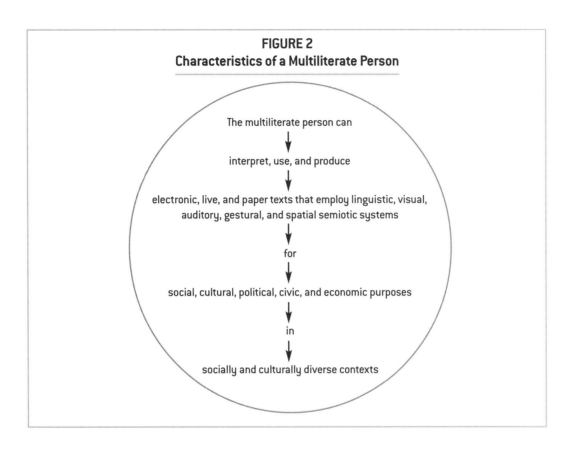

FIGURE 2
Characteristics of a Multiliterate Person

The multiliterate person can

↓

interpret, use, and produce

↓

electronic, live, and paper texts that employ linguistic, visual,
auditory, gestural, and spatial semiotic systems

↓

for

↓

social, cultural, political, civic, and economic purposes

↓

in

↓

socially and culturally diverse contexts

and be able to do?' Freebody and Luke asked this question in 1990 when they were trying to explore ways of balancing a reading curriculum. They developed a model called the Four Roles of the Reader that was originally intended to inform the teaching of reading, but more recently Freebody and Luke (2003) have written about the four roles as a model for literacy teaching and learning. Therefore, we have presented this model as a way of balancing the planning and teaching of multiliteracies.

Understanding the Four Resource Model

The Four Roles of the Reader model has undergone a number of name changes since Freebody and Luke first published their work in 1990. It is more recently referred to as the Four Resource Model (Anstey, 2002b), which outlines the reader practices *code breaker*, *meaning maker*, *text user*, and *text analyst*. The title Four Resource Model is most appropriate here because it focuses on literacy rather than reading and because the use of the term *resource* reminds teachers that students will be able to engage in the four reading practices only if they are able to identify and use the appropriate resources.

A multiliterate person should approach literacy as a problem-solving activity that involves analysing the context and purpose of the task, deciding on a plan of action, and identifying and accessing appropriate resources (see Figure 3). As the person engages in the literacy task, he or she should self-monitor and note if the approach is successful or if the strategy needs to be reviewed and modified. If developing multiliterate students is the goal of literacy teaching, then teachers need a way of identifying the different purposes for engaging in literate practices and the resources that might be needed for each purpose. Teachers also need to identify pedagogies that teach students to analyse tasks, problem solve, identify resources, and self-monitor. Therefore, rather than mainly focussing on lists of content in the multiliteracies program (the what), planning for the teaching of multiliteracies needs

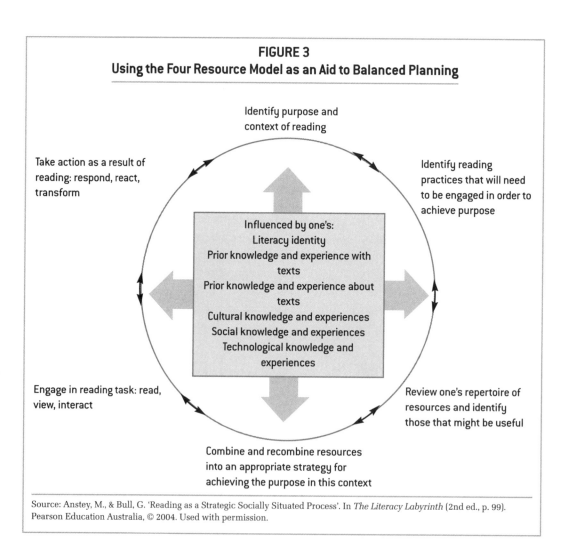

FIGURE 3
Using the Four Resource Model as an Aid to Balanced Planning

Identify purpose and context of reading

Take action as a result of reading: respond, react, transform

Identify reading practices that will need to be engaged in order to achieve purpose

Influenced by one's:
Literacy identity
Prior knowledge and experience with texts
Prior knowledge and experience about texts
Cultural knowledge and experiences
Social knowledge and experiences
Technological knowledge and experiences

Engage in reading task: read, view, interact

Review one's repertoire of resources and identify those that might be useful

Combine and recombine resources into an appropriate strategy for achieving the purpose in this context

Source: Anstey, M., & Bull, G. 'Reading as a Strategic Socially Situated Process'. In *The Literacy Labyrinth* (2nd ed., p. 99). Pearson Education Australia, © 2004. Used with permission.

to focus equally on how the literate practice is done for different purposes and in different contexts. If teachers focus only on lists of content (the what) the result is a static view of literacy that focuses on one set of skills that can be applied in a range of contexts without change. This approach does not focus on literacy as a social practice, nor does it focus on the transformative nature of multiliteracies required in a changing world, where citizens actively engage with and design their social futures. Therefore, the literacy curriculum must focus on the what and the how.

When A. Luke and Freebody (1997) developed the Four Roles of the Reader as an approach to the teaching of reading, they focused on the question, 'What are the kinds of reading practices and positions schools should value, encourage, and propagate?' (p. 213). To answer this question, they attempted to identify and describe the way individuals use reading as part of their everyday lives by asking three further questions:

1. What are the practices of reading engaged in?
2. What do these practices demand of the reader?
3. What resources are needed in order to engage in these practices?

Luke and Freebody advocated starting with the reading practices individuals engage in, so the focus would remain on how reading is constructed and enacted in all aspects of life. Because the focus is on use of reading practices, rather than on texts or skills, the school reading program can respond to the particular needs of a school community and change with those needs. There is little chance that any particular text, culture, or practice would be excluded or included. Therefore, any voice or text from any context could be read, analysed, critiqued, or reconstructed. In this way the reading program would value the knowledge that students from diverse backgrounds bring to schools.

All these questions and statements apply equally to the development of a multiliteracies curriculum. For example, Luke and Freebody's (1997) three questions could be modified thus:

1. What are the literate practices engaged in?
2. What do these practices demand of the multiliterate person?
3. What resources are needed in order to engage in these literate practices?

After examining their three questions, Luke and Freebody developed the Four Roles of the Reader as a framework to help teachers interpret the social critical theories of literacy specifically in terms of the teaching of reading. They identified four practices of reading and suggested that in order to engage in these reading practices, readers drew on a repertoire of resources.

These resources would be the literacy, social, cultural, and technological knowledge and experience that make up the reader's literacy identity. Some of these resources might be used for particular practices, but many would be used across several practices. An explanation of each of the practices and the resources that assist in using those practices follows.

Code Breaker

The practice of code breaking refers to a person's ability to identify and use the semiotic systems in electronic, paper, and live texts. That is, a student needs to be able to make sense of the marks on the page in the case of a print-on-paper text, or the gestures, facial expression, pitch, tone, and volume in the case of a live text, such as a discussion. Many texts are multimodal, drawing on more than one semiotic system. Therefore, the practice of code breaking must also involve working out how the different semiotic systems in the text work on their own and in combination with others. For example, in a moving image the auditory semiotic system works in combination with the semiotics of moving images. In many electronic and paper texts the linguistic semiotic system of words and sentences work in combination with the visual semiotics of still images such as illustrations, photos, charts, and graphs. In order to be literate with these texts, a person must first be able to break the code. The resources essential to practicing code breaking are knowledge about all five semiotic systems and how different texts work.

THEORY INTO PRACTICE: CLASSROOM APPLICATION

In order to focus students on code-breaking practices when engaging with literate activities, use the following questions for discussion about the literate activities about to be engaged in. They can be modified for different age groups, but the term *code breaking* should be used with all age groups so that students begin to associate the practice with that term.

1. Ask a general opening question:
   ‣ What types of texts (electronic, paper, or live) are we using in this literate practice, and what do we know about them?

2. Ask questions about code breaking each text:
   ‣ How do we crack this text?
   ‣ What modes does it use (e.g., oral or written)?
   ‣ Is there more than one semiotic system operating here?
   ‣ What do we know about the codes and conventions of each of these semiotic systems?

> ▸▸ How do the semiotic systems in this text relate to one another?

> ▸▸ Which should I attend to first and which should I look at in relation to each other (e.g., relationship between words [linguistic] and charts [visual])?

3. Ask questions about how the text works:

> ▸▸ Is there a generic structure? If so, what does it look like and how might it help us?

> ▸▸ Is there a particular layout or organisation that will help us?

> ▸▸ Is there a specialised vocabulary that is used in texts like this that I need to know?

Meaning Maker

Meaning-making practices are used to make literal and inferential meanings of texts. In order to do this, a student must draw on and use meaning-making resources and code-breaking resources. The student's literacy identity—all previous literacy, social, cultural, and technological experiences—is the major resource for meaning making. The context in which the literacy activity takes place also influences meaning making.

Because literacy identity is so influential to meaning-making practices, it is important for students to understand that different groups may make different meanings of text because of their different social or cultural backgrounds. Some cultures and social groups access particular genres and practice literacy in particular ways. This may mean that some people will have different resources to draw on and will be more competent in some situations and less competent in others. For example, narratives in western cultures often have a pattern of three (e.g., three wishes, three attempts to achieve a goal, three little pigs, three bears), but in some Pacific Island cultures narratives have a pattern of four. If cultural background leads a student to expect a pattern of four in narratives, consider how this would influence the student's meaning making with western narratives, where the pattern of three is common. In this situation, the student could give up and say, 'I am not competent', or look at the resources he or she does have and use them strategically. For example, rather than giving up, the student might try something like this: Having identified the text as a narrative (using his or her resources about generic structures) the person would then use the characteristic of a pattern of four (because this is part of his or her resources about narrative). However, when this pattern does not work, a multiliterate person would then look to see if another pattern appears to be operating in the text. In this way, the student might work out the pattern of three. Meaning making is not simply about having or not having the resources; it is about knowing how to adapt or recombine them or use a strategy to work out how to use the resources already acquired. Some groups prefer to read information text rather than narrative. When these groups encounter narrative, they have fewer or different resources to draw on to make meaning of it. But if they use their resources well, they will still be able to make meaning.

THEORY INTO PRACTICE: CLASSROOM APPLICATION

In order to focus students on the meaning-making practices when engaging with literate activities, use the following questions for discussion. They can be modified for different age groups, but the term *meaning making* should be used with all age groups so that students begin to associate the practice with that term.

1. If the purpose and context require making literal meanings or drawing inferences, ask, 'What prior knowledge and experiences might help me make meaning of this text?'

   Prior Experience With Texts and Knowledge About Texts
   - Have you seen a text like this before?
   - Where was it?
   - What was it used for?
   - How did you use it?
   - What characteristics of that text are similar or different to this one?
   - How would that affect the way you will use this text for this purpose?
   - Is this a genre you have used before?
   - What is this genre generally used for?
   - If this text is similar in structure to a particular genre, how might that help you use this text?

   Cultural and Social Knowledge and Experience
   - Have you used texts like this in similar contexts?
   - How did you behave with the text in those contexts?
   - Have you interacted with people before when engaging in this type of task?
   - How might this previous experience help you here?
   - What do you know about this social or cultural group (or context) that might help you work out the best way of going about this task?

Text User

The focus of text user practices is the use of text in real-life situations. These situations usually involve several participants but on occasion may be solitary. Examples include negotiations around a written text, such as service encounters in banks or government agencies (which might be done face to face or over the Internet), using instructions to assemble a piece of furniture, or working on a collaborative task in the workplace. Text user activities might occur in workplace, leisure, religious, or other social settings, and these contexts would influence how the practice took place. For example, the use of instructions to assemble something collaboratively in the workplace would differ from such an activity at home or among friends.

As with other literate practices, text user practices often require the use of multiple modes (listening, speaking, reading, viewing, and writing) and semiotic systems (linguistic, visual, auditory, gestural, and spatial). The text user might also work with multiple types of texts (electronic, paper, live) either simultaneously or at different times during the task. For example, a text user task, such as deciding on and signing up for a new mobile phone plan, could involve a paper text such as a brochure, a live text such as discussing options with the sales assistant, and a jointly constructed online text as the purchaser provides oral information to the sales assistant, who enters the contract information into the computer.

Therefore, knowing about texts, their purpose, structure, and use is very important to text user activities. The text user needs to understand that although the text might have the same purpose in different contexts and on different platforms, the structure or layout might vary, and slightly different behaviours and oral interactions might be expected when using the text. The following example from Anstey and Bull (2004) illustrates this point. The retelling of an event might use the same generic structure across different contexts and platforms, but in those different situations it will contain different semiotic systems and require different ways of participating. If the purpose of the retelling is to entertain (an anecdote) it might be conducted in a face-to-face oral encounter while viewing a person's holiday photos, accompanied by exaggerated intonation, facial expressions, and gestures. If the retelling is for a news report on television, viewers might see the news presenter reading part of the item, then a video clip and voice-over, followed by a brief interview between a reporter and a person at the site of the news event. Although the purpose of both situations is retelling, and the generic structure of the retelling would be similar, the role of the text user and participant is quite different in the two cases. In the first retelling, the text user would be expected to laugh, ask further questions, or make a comment about the anecdote and photos. In the second situation, the text user would be more passive, not interacting with the news report but possibly engaging in a conversation about it while viewing it with someone else. In these two cases, the purposes and contexts are different, the semiotic systems are different, and the behaviours required are different, but the genre of the texts (a recount) is the same. Knowing and recognising the genre is insufficient to function as a text user. The student must draw on other practices (code breaking and meaning making) and other aspects of his or her literacy identity (social and cultural background and experiences) in order to complete text user activities successfully.

Text user practices are an extremely important element in the literacy program, as they play a major part in people's everyday lives. Most literate tasks are pragmatic activities; that is, their purpose is to get something done.

THEORY INTO PRACTICE: CLASSROOM APPLICATION

In order to focus students on being strategic when engaging with text user activities, teachers can explore questions students might use to devise a strategy. They can be modified for different age groups, but the term *text user* should be used with all age groups so that students begin to associate the practice with that term.

1. Ask opening questions to focus on the aim of the task and the context:
    ▸▸ What is my purpose—what am I trying to achieve?
    ▸▸ Who is involved, and where am I doing this?

2. Ask questions about the texts that might be used:

- ▸▸ What texts are being used (e.g., paper, electronic, live)?
- ▸▸ Are the texts used for different purposes (e.g., a paper brochure to provide information, live oral text as a vehicle for negotiation or discussion, an electronic form to be filled in to legalise a contract)?
- ▸▸ How do the purpose and use of each text shape its composition—what genres can I expect to encounter?
- ▸▸ What do I know about these genres that will help me with this task?

3. Ask questions about behaviour:

- ▸▸ Who are the participants in this task, what is my relationship with them, and how will this affect my behaviour?
- ▸▸ How will this affect my use of language (both oral and written, e.g., choice of vocabulary)?
- ▸▸ What is my role and what is theirs?
- ▸▸ What should I do with each text used in this context; what is my role with each text?
- ▸▸ What will others do with each text, and what is their role?
- ▸▸ What are my options or alternatives after completing this text user task?

Text Analyst

Text analyst practices involve the critical analysis of literacy activities and the texts used in them in order to make informed decisions about how to behave and use the texts that are a part of the literacy activity. A large part of being a proficient text analyst is understanding how texts construct and reconstruct people's perceptions of the world, and how texts potentially shape people's behaviours and how they live and the power they exercise over their lives. Being a text analyst helps a person have control over his or her own future. The person engaging in text analyst practices, rather than the text and other participants, holds the power. That person will decide how to participate and use the text and what authority to accord it and the other participants.

An important part of being a text analyst is understanding how texts (live, paper, and electronic) are constructed and produced. Therefore, in order to engage in text analyst practices, students must draw on resources from all four practices of the Four Resource Model. Code-breaking skills are used to reflect on how the use of different semiotic systems shapes meaning and what meanings are being conveyed by particular semiotic systems. For example, the use of a visual image can be more influential than words. Similarly, linguistic code-breaking skills, such as understanding about layout and organisation of texts and the use of colour, font, and size of headings, are useful when reflecting on how meaning is being shaped. In terms of live texts, code-breaking skills applied to the gestural and auditory semiotic systems are important, for example, understanding how pitch, volume, body position, and facial expression can position the student in a literacy activity. Meaning-making resources, such as reflecting on prior knowledge and experience and how that positions the student to interact with the text and other participants, are important to critical analysis. Similarly, text user resources are helpful in considering the purpose and context of the literate activity, the genres the student might encounter and their characteristics, and the behaviours expected. Once again, having thought about these aspects critically, students can adjust their behaviour and be prepared for the situation, ensuring that they are empowered.

The examples of using resources from all four practices also demonstrate how they can aid in the identification and analysis of values in texts. In some texts the values are more overt than others. Generally the audience can easily recognise advertising material as a text that is obviously constructed with a particular purpose and that follows a particular structure. However, sometimes other genres are used that disguise the fact that the purpose of the text is advertising. They also disguise the fact that the author is the advertised product's producer, and therefore the text will be produced in a particular way. For example, we often see television and print advertising presented as a scientific report but with a tiny notation stating that it is an advertisement. More recently, companies such as BMW have employed well-known directors and movie stars to make short movies for viewing on their website or for purchase on DVD. These are legitimate short movies, but they prominently feature BMW cars in ways that show off their capabilities. Their purpose is to advertise. Junk mail or advertising catalogues at particular times of year present views of gender, parenting, family structures, and cultural and religious celebrations through the gifts they put in the foreground. They also portray families and celebrations in particular ways. For example, particular socioeconomic groups and family structures might be included or excluded.

The text analyst practices of critical literacy should not be limited to an analysis of the media and popular culture such as movies, magazines, websites, and novels. Business documents and information sheets that seem innocuous also convey values and ideologies and empower and disempower either the producer or user. For example, loan agreements and rental or insurance contracts may use phrases that are open to interpretation, such as 'in a reasonable time.' The oral (live) texts of literate activities should be examined as well. For example, consider a meeting situation in which two groups of people need to negotiate a contract. The text analyst would think about how space is used and how participants are positioned in relation to each other.

Is there a desk in between the two parties, are all the chairs the same—higher or lower, more or less difficult to sit in and appear at ease? The analyst would consider body language, gesture, and dress—and whether they are being used to position people in particular ways. Finally, the analyst would examine what language is being used—is it common, or is specialised, obtuse language being used that favours one group?

The most important aspect of being a text analyst is what the person does after critically analysing the texts (live, paper, electronic) of the literate activity. Being a text analyst means being an active and informed citizen and taking control of one's life. This occurs only if the text analyst takes action as a result of the analysis. This action is called engaging in transformation. Having critically analysed the texts, the person should then consider the action to take as a result of the analyses. For example, if a contract has phrases that are open to interpretation, the analyst might seek clarification and perhaps request rephrasing or adding a clarifying statement to the contract. Another example would be someone arriving at a meeting to find that chairs and tables are positioned in a way that puts him or her in a less powerful position. The analyst might take action to move them or sit in the powerful seat if all are vacant. If these tactics are not possible, then the analyst would remain aware of his or her positioning and not be intimidated as the meeting proceeds. If people are deliberately using obtuse language, the analyst would stop them politely and suggest using a shared language to achieve the meeting's goal. Similarly, a student who finds an advertisement offensive might contact company officials and tell them so or might exercise the right to purchase the same type of product from another company. A student who uses text analyst practices might enjoy the movies or read the science reports that are actually advertising, but still remember that they are advertising and be able to resist their influence.

THEORY INTO PRACTICE: CLASSROOM APPLICATION

Because transformation is such a critical part of text analyst practices, it is important that planning and pedagogy with text analyst literacy practices involve students in taking action (transformation) as a result of their analyses. Therefore, the questions suggested here as ways of discussing how to engage in text analyst practices include discussions about transformation (action).

1. Ask opening questions to focus on the aim of the task and the context:
   ▸▸ What is the purpose of this literate activity, and what is trying to be achieved?

- ▸▸ Who is involved and with what interests and values?
- ▸▸ Why am I involved—what are my purposes, interests, and values?
- ▸▸ Is there social or cultural knowledge or experience that will assist me in this situation?

2. Ask questions about the texts that might be used:
- ▸▸ What texts are being used (e.g., paper, electronic, live)?
- ▸▸ What are the origins of this text, who authored it, and what authority does the author have?
- ▸▸ How do the origins of this text affect the way in which I should position myself when I read it?
- ▸▸ Are the texts used for different purposes, and what are they?
- ▸▸ How does the purpose and use of each text shape its composition—what genres can I expect to encounter?
- ▸▸ What do I know about these genres and texts that will help me identify dominant positions and beliefs?
- ▸▸ What do I know about these genres and texts that will help me identify beliefs and positions that are being silenced?

3. Ask questions about transformation:
- ▸▸ What is my desired relationship with the participants in this literate activity, and how will I behave?
- ▸▸ How will this affect my use of language (both oral and written, e.g., choice of vocabulary)?
- ▸▸ What do I think about the text of this literate activity, and what action should I take?
- ▸▸ What is the text trying to make me believe and do?
- ▸▸ What alternatives are there to the beliefs and ideas presented in this text?
- ▸▸ How might I reconstruct or modify this text as I participate in this literate activity?
- ▸▸ What actions will I take as a result of my analyses?

Planning With the Four Resource Model

The Four Resource Model provides teachers with a way of balancing their multiliteracies curriculum in terms of content, pedagogy, and assessment to ensure that they are teaching all practices of multiliteracies. It also helps teachers provide students with knowledge, strategies, problem-solving skills, and a language to interrogate, produce, and use the texts they will encounter now and in the future. It encourages the teaching of literacy from a social–critical perspective that is responsive to change.

Figure 4 presents just one way in which the Four Resource Model might be used as an aid in planning for the teaching of multiliteracies. As can be seen in Figure 4, the Four Resource Model can inform the selection and analysis of texts to be used, and aid teachers in identifying specific knowledge and resources that students will need to engage with those texts at various stages of the unit. This advance work can then inform the planning of specific lessons and the selection of appropriate pedagogy. In this way teachers can be sure that they are teaching multiliteracies in a balanced way, addressing all four practices and the resources readers need to engage in them, and exploring all types of texts—live, paper, and electronic.

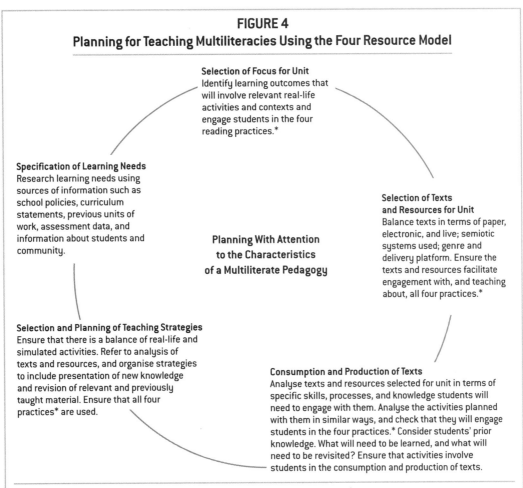

FIGURE 4
Planning for Teaching Multiliteracies Using the Four Resource Model

Selection of Focus for Unit
Identify learning outcomes that will involve relevant real-life activities and contexts and engage students in the four reading practices.*

Specification of Learning Needs
Research learning needs using sources of information such as school policies, curriculum statements, previous units of work, assessment data, and information about students and community.

Planning With Attention to the Characteristics of a Multiliterate Pedagogy

Selection of Texts and Resources for Unit
Balance texts in terms of paper, electronic, and live; semiotic systems used; genre and delivery platform. Ensure the texts and resources facilitate engagement with, and teaching about, all four practices.*

Selection and Planning of Teaching Strategies
Ensure that there is a balance of real-life and simulated activities. Refer to analysis of texts and resources, and organise strategies to include presentation of new knowledge and revision of relevant and previously taught material. Ensure that all four practices* are used.

Consumption and Production of Texts
Analyse texts and resources selected for unit in terms of specific skills, processes, and knowledge students will need to engage with them. Analyse the activities planned with them in similar ways, and check that they will engage students in the four practices.* Consider students' prior knowledge. What will need to be learned, and what will need to be revisited? Ensure that activities involve students in the consumption and production of texts.

* The four reading practices are code breaker, meaning maker, text user, and text analyst.

FIGURE 5
A Suggested Procedure for Analysing Texts

Text Details
Title of text ....
Type of text (i.e., live, electronic, paper) ....
Semiotic systems used ....
Delivery platform (e.g., CD-ROM, website) ....

Analysis of Text
Genres (there may be more than one) in text ....
Purpose of text ....
Context in which used ....
Learning purpose with text (e.g., identify point of view) ....

Practices Used to Complete Task With Text	Resources Needed to Engage in Practice	
	What Students Need to Know (Knowing What to Do)	What Students Need to Be Able to Do (Knowing How to Do It)
Code breaker		
Meaning maker		
Text user		
Text analyst		

Source: Anstey, M. *Literate Futures: Reading* (p. 43). State of Queensland Department of Education, © 2002. Used with permission.

As can be seen in Figure 5, teachers should analyse the texts to be used in a unit of work to ensure that they are aware of the resources needed to engage with those texts. Figure 5 provides a suggested framework for analysing texts.

Summary: Connecting Literacy and Multiliteracies

The beginning of this chapter explored the characteristics of a literate person:

>> *flexible*—is positive and strategically responsive to changing literacies;

>> able to *sustain mastery*—knows enough to be able to reformulate current knowledge or access and learn new literate practices;

- has a *repertoire of practices*—has a range of knowledge, skills, and strategies to use when appropriate;
- able to *use traditional texts*—can use print and paper, face-to-face oral encounters; and
- able to *use new communications technologies*—can use digital and electronic texts that use multiple modes, often simultaneously.

As noted earlier, these characteristics of literacy are also embedded in multiliteracies, along with other dimensions. The concept of multiliteracies focusses on how literacy and literate practices have been influenced by local and global, social, cultural, and technological change. Teachers particularly should help students explore the changing nature of texts and develop understandings about text. Therefore, in the context of literacy education, the goal of achieving multiliteracies involves pedagogy as much as literacy. Teachers of multiliteracies are preparing students for social futures in which they actively participate and influence their social futures, that is, in which they are the designers of their social futures.

Multiliteracies focus on

- technology and the increase of multimedia texts;
- the influence of increasing social, cultural, and linguistic diversity on literacy and literate practices; and
- critical literacy.

Therefore, as Anstey (2003) explains, a multiliterate person is flexible and strategic and can understand and use literacy and literate practices

- with a range of texts and technologies;
- in socially responsible ways;
- in a socially, culturally, and linguistically diverse world; and
- to fully participate in life as an active and informed citizen.

These characteristics can help guide teachers' planning and pedagogy. Chapter 3 examines how teachers can develop their pedagogy to teach multiliteracies and prepare students for current and future literacies.

CHAPTER 3

Developing Pedagogies for Multiliteracies

This chapter explores the implications of multiliteracies in terms of pedagogical change, so teachers can identify characteristics of pedagogy that will assist students in becoming multiliterate. It commences by identifying principles for guiding the development of a multiliteracies curriculum. Conclusions from recent research about literacy pedagogy are reviewed. Teachers will also find specific guidelines for lesson development and ways of reviewing teaching practices with a view to developing pedagogies for multiliteracies.

Principles for a Multiliteracies Curriculum

In order to arrive at a set of principles to guide the development of a multiliteracies curriculum, it is necessary to examine relationships between the characteristics of a literate person, multiliteracies, and the characteristics of a multiliterate person. These characteristics and definitions were reviewed at the end of chapter 2. By examining the links between being literate and multiliterate, teachers can extrapolate the characteristics of a multiliteracies curriculum (see Figure 6). Broadly, a multiliteracies curriculum must provide opportunities for students to explore, learn about, and engage with literacy and literate practices. Teachers can use the following set of points as guiding principles for developing a multiliteracies curriculum, if they preface them with the stem question 'Does my curriculum include _____?':

- ▸▸ exploration and use of literacy and literate practices in a balance of known and unknown, authentic, and simulated contexts;
- ▸▸ opportunities to consume, produce, and transform knowledge about literacy and literate practices;
- ▸▸ opportunities to investigate and develop understandings about how literate practices operate and relate in the social, cultural, political, economic, and ideological world;

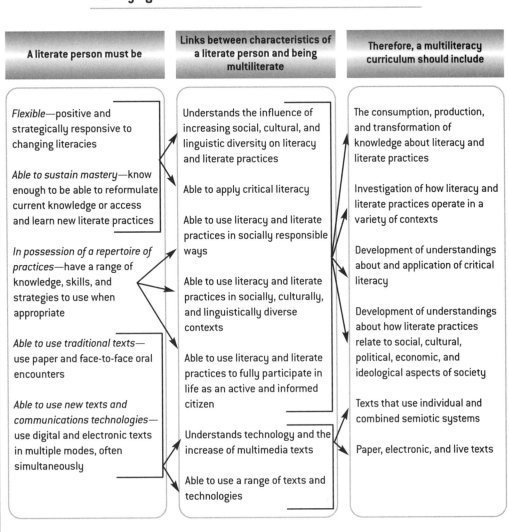

FIGURE 6
Identifying the Characteristics of a Multiliterate Curriculum

A literate person must be	Links between characteristics of a literate person and being multiliterate	Therefore, a multiliteracy curriculum should include
Flexible—positive and strategically responsive to changing literacies	Understands the influence of increasing social, cultural, and linguistic diversity on literacy and literate practices	The consumption, production, and transformation of knowledge about literacy and literate practices
Able to sustain mastery—know enough to be able to reformulate current knowledge or access and learn new literate practices	Able to apply critical literacy Able to use literacy and literate practices in socially responsible ways	Investigation of how literacy and literate practices operate in a variety of contexts
In possession of a repertoire of practices—have a range of knowledge, skills, and strategies to use when appropriate	Able to use literacy and literate practices in socially, culturally, and linguistically diverse contexts	Development of understandings about and application of critical literacy
Able to use traditional texts—use paper and face-to-face oral encounters	Able to use literacy and literate practices to fully participate in life as an active and informed citizen	Development of understandings about how literate practices relate to social, cultural, political, economic, and ideological aspects of society
Able to use new texts and communications technologies—use digital and electronic texts in multiple modes, often simultaneously	Understands technology and the increase of multimedia texts Able to use a range of texts and technologies	Texts that use individual and combined semiotic systems Paper, electronic, and live texts

- ▸▸ the development of understandings about and application of critical literacy skills;
- ▸▸ opportunities to learn about, interpret, and produce texts that use individual and combined semiotic systems (linguistic, visual, auditory, spatial, and gestural); and
- ▸▸ opportunities to learn about, interpret, and produce paper, electronic, and live texts.

The successful teaching of multiliteracies is not achieved simply by applying guiding principles to identify content and contexts for learning about literacy and literate practices. Rather, much of the success in teaching multiliteracies lies in developing pedagogies that facilitate the type of learning required. In doing that, teachers should keep the goal in mind—the development of a multiliterate person who is strategic and flexible, has a range of resources available, and can combine them and recombine them for different purposes and contexts. Simply teaching content and skills will not achieve this goal. A multiliterate pedagogy requires teaching the thinking, behavioural, and social skills that are associated with being multiliterate. Researchers have found that achieving this sort of balance between content, thinking, behavioural, and social skills requires a dynamic pedagogy.

Investigating Pedagogy

Research regarding pedagogy, in particular literacy pedagogy, since the 1990s has focussed on the following areas:

- ▶▶ the intellectual and social demands of classroom pedagogies,
- ▶▶ the classroom as a social environment,
- ▶▶ relationships among social and cultural diversity and pedagogy,
- ▶▶ classroom practices,
- ▶▶ the way talk is conducted in the classroom, and
- ▶▶ the ways in which knowledge is constructed in classrooms.

Intellectual Demands of Classroom Pedagogies

The first piece of research to be discussed examined pedagogy at a more general level and has implications for the planning of our pedagogy. The Queensland School Reform Longitudinal Study conducted from 1998 to 2000 and reported in Land (2001) identified areas of pedagogy that needed to change in order to achieve improved student outcomes. It concluded that levels of intellectual demand and social support are both linked to improved outcomes. What was most interesting, however, were the findings that the levels of social support were already generally in place, but the intellectual demand of classroom pedagogy could be improved. Students were provided with very supportive learning environments and teachers were very nurturing. In terms of the intellectual demand of classrooms, researchers found that the focus was more on developing basic skills than engaging students in higher order thinking. Students were asked to recall facts and engage in simple routines more often than to transform information and ideas. If we interpret this finding in terms of the Four Resource Model discussed in chapter 2, the results show that students were engaged more frequently in code-breaking and meaning-making practices than in text user or text analyst practices. Because of this, students were less likely to develop deep understandings and knowledge about concepts that they could have used in strategic and flexible ways for other purposes and in other contexts. These findings led to the identification of four areas in which pedagogy should be examined and improved in order to achieve better outcomes. Called Productive Pedagogies, these four areas were (1) intellectual quality, (2) connectedness, (3) supportive classroom environment, and (4) recognition of difference. Within these areas, researchers identified a total of 20 specific items for attention. In Table 1 these

TABLE 1
Interpreting the Productive Pedagogies for a Multiliterate Pedagogy

Productive Pedagogies	Applied to a Multiliteracies Pedagogy
Intellectual Quality	
Higher order thinking, deep knowledge, deep understanding	• Learning about literacy and literate practices, how paper, live, and electronic texts and the five semiotic systems work in social, cultural, economic, and political contexts.
Substantive conversation	• Talk in the classroom should go beyond question-and-answer sequences and involve students in conversations about how literacy works.
Knowledge as problematic	• Literacy should be viewed as changing rather than static, and there should be an emphasis on strategic thinking and problem-solving approaches to literacy tasks. The development of metacognitive skills should be a feature of all literacy lessons.
Metalanguage	• Students and teachers develop a language for talking about literacy; that is, appropriate terminology should be learned and used in all conversations about literacy.
Connectedness	
Knowledge integration, connectedness to the world	• Literacy teaching and learning should be situated in real contexts and use authentic texts, incorporating all disciplines.
Background knowledge	• The literacy identities of students should be recognised to ensure teaching and learning activities are relevant and meaningful to students and acknowledge student diversity.
Problem-based curriculum	• Classroom activities and discussion should emphasise strategic thinking and problem solving as a way of engaging with real-life literate tasks using authentic texts.

(continued)

TABLE 1 (continued)
Interpreting the Productive Pedagogies for a Multiliterate Pedagogy

Productive Pedagogies	Applied to a Multiliteracies Pedagogy
Supportive Classroom Environment	
Student direction	• Students have the opportunity to identify literate practices they would like to investigate.
Social support	• Provide social support through mutual respect and acknowledgment of students' own interests and literate practices.
Academic engagement, explicit quality performance criteria	• Teachers and students have a shared understanding of the expected levels and nature of participation in literacy lessons, and knowledge and performance outcomes for literacy learning are clearly specified.
Self-regulation	• As part of the focus on problem solving, strategic thinking, and metacognition, students engage in critical reflection on their literacy learning through discussion or reflection journals.
Recognition of Difference	
Cultural knowledge, inclusivity, group identity	• Teachers identify the literate practices of their students and the social and cultural influences on their literate practices (i.e., their literacy identity) to ensure teaching and learning activities are relevant and meaningful to students and acknowledge their diversity.
Narrative	• Narrative (oral or written) is used as a way of talking about and investigating literacy. It is also used as a metacognitive tool, to reflect on how a task was completed or might be completed.
Active citizenship	• Because literacy teaching and learning is situated in real contexts and uses authentic texts, students develop an understanding about the role of literacy in being an active and informed citizen with power over one's future.

Source: Anstey, M., & Bull, G. *The Literacy Labyrinth* (2nd ed., p. 314). Pearson Education Australia, © 2004. Used with permission.

Productive Pedagogies (Land, 2001; Lingard, Hayes, & Mills, 2003; Lingard, Hayes, Mills, & Christie, 2003) have been explained in terms of their implications for a multiliteracies pedagogy.

The implications of this research for developing a pedagogy for multiliteracies are many, but two areas are particularly significant. First, the characteristics of a multiliterate person indicate an ability to engage in higher order thinking, using deep knowledge and understandings in new and different ways. These characteristics also indicate that such a person needs to be flexible in order to understand that literacy and literate practices are dynamic not static, and that they change as a result of social, cultural, and technological change. In terms of the Productive Pedagogies, a multiliterate person views knowledge as problematic. Two of the Productive Pedagogies, intellectual quality and connectedness, provide guidelines for the intellectual aspects of a multiliteracies pedagogy. The second area that is significant is the necessity to achieve a balance between the intellectual and supportive aspects of a teacher's pedagogy. Once again the 4 areas and 20 items of the Productive Pedagogies provide guidance here. If teachers consider their planning and pedagogy in terms of the areas in Table 1, they can be somewhat assured that they will achieve this balance. Furthermore, combining attention to the Productive Pedagogies and the Four Resource Model ensures that lower order and higher order thinking skills are addressed (i.e., code breaking and meaning making as well as text user and text analyst practices). By including all these elements, teachers will have a pedagogy that is dynamic rather than static and that addresses multiliteracies.

THEORY INTO PRACTICE: CLASSROOM APPLICATION

One way of applying the Productive Pedagogies is to use the ideas presented in Table 1 to reflect on your planning for teaching and pedagogy. Try the following tasks.

1. Identify a concept that you are about to start teaching over the next few weeks, for example, finding the main idea in a text, drawing conclusions, making inferences, or teaching about a new genre. Now explore the teaching of this concept in terms of intellectual quality, specifically, higher order thinking, and deep understanding. (Check this part of Table 1 before you begin.)

   ▸▸ List the knowledge and understandings involved with that concept. What will your students need to know and be able to do?

   ▸▸ Categorise this knowledge and understanding into lower order thinking skills (e.g., recall a sequence of events) and higher order thinking skills (identify and explain how the point of view is constructed in the text).

   ▸▸ Think about the ways in which you will teach this concept to ensure that lower order and higher order thinking skills are taught.

The following example shows how this might apply to planning a sequence of lessons on finding information in a text. (This could apply to an electronic text or a written text, but clearly knowledge about how electronic texts are accessed and engaged with would need to be added.) This example is not meant to be exhaustive but to aid you in understanding the application of these ideas.

List the knowledge and understandings involved with the concept of *finding information in a text*. What will your students need to know and be able to do?	▶▶ Purpose for reading; what they need to find out. ▶▶ Specialised vocabulary associated with that idea or concept. ▶▶ Cohesive ties that might link or point to that information (e.g., *because, therefore, and, but,* etc.). ▶▶ Aspects of layout and font that might draw attention to information (e.g., size, colour, bold, underline, italics, numbering, bullet points). ▶▶ Knowledge and application of generic structures that might help identify where information is most likely to be found. ▶▶ Knowledge of paragraphing that might help identify where information is most likely to be found (e.g., topic sentences). ▶▶ The use and purpose of images, diagrams, and other visual material.
Categorise this knowledge and understanding into lower order thinking skills and higher order thinking skills.	**Lower order thinking skills** ▶▶ Aspects of layout and font that might draw attention to information (e.g., size, colour, bold, underline, italics, numbering, bullet points). ▶▶ Specialised vocabulary associated with that idea or concept. ▶▶ Knowledge of paragraphing that might help identify where information is most likely to be found (e.g., topic sentences). ▶▶ The use and purpose of images, diagrams, and other visual material. **Higher order thinking skills** ▶▶ Purpose for reading; what they need to find out. ▶▶ Knowledge and application of generic structures that might help identify where information is most likely to be found.
Think about the ways in which you will teach this concept in order to ensure both lower order and higher order thinking skills are taught.	**Lower order thinking skills** As lower order thinking skills have previously been taught, we will revise these concepts and then talk about their application in the context of how they might be used to find information. **Higher order thinking skills** ▶▶ Concentrated discussion on different purposes for reading and the need to remain focussed on purpose in order to identify best strategy ▶▶ Compare–contrast chart: Examine a number of different purposes for reading and what they entail, their focus, what they demand of readers. Compare a few tasks and how they would require different strategies. (Refer to revision lessons with lower order thinking skills.) Develop a chart as summary to reinforce that different tasks require different strategies.

2. Explore the teaching of the concept you have chosen in terms of intellectual quality, specifically, metalanguage (see Table 1 on pages 59–60).

   ‣ What specific terminology and language will be used in teaching this concept?

   ‣ List terminology and define each term to ensure you can explain it to the students.

   ‣ Check that this is the terminology used throughout the school and curriculum documents, so all are consistent.

   ‣ Which of these terms will be familiar to your students and which will be new?

   ‣ How will you introduce or revise these terms? What references will you provide for students to use later?

The Classroom as a Social Environment: Addressing Diversity

A number of researchers have examined the classroom as a specific social environment in which talk and social interactions are conducted in particular ways and there are shared meanings and understandings among participants that are unique to the school context. Much of what goes on in schools occurs through oral interactions between teacher and students, that is, through talk. The ways in which this talk is conducted can advantage and disadvantage students, particularly given students' social and cultural diversity as well as their diverse learning abilities. The research indicates that there are two major ways in which students can be disadvantaged by the social interaction of the classroom. The first is to do with the acculturating function of schooling, and the second is to do with the often implicit pedagogy that is used.

The Acculturing Factor in the Classroom

Baker (1991b) and Heap (1985) suggest that classroom discourse has an acculturating function. It transmits not only general knowledge but also knowledge about how the culture of the school and its community operates. If some students in the class come from a social or cultural group that is in the minority of the school and its community, it is possible that they will be disadvantaged or excluded. They might be unfamiliar with the social and cultural practices that have influenced the way in which school routines and interactions are conducted; they don't know the rules of engagement. Louden and Rivalland (1995) studied the literacy practices of students from different ethnic, cultural, and social backgrounds in Western Australia and how these practices were reflected in the way their schools practiced literacy. One group of students' cultural and religious literate practices with text were mostly about remembering and repeating word for word what they had read (code breaking and meaning making). Therefore, when they entered the classroom and the interactions around text required a different kind of participation, based more on text user and text analyst literate practices, they had some difficulty.

This is not a new finding. Heath (1982) found that parents and students of minority groups in white middle class classrooms were aware that the literate practices and interactions of their homes differed from those in the classroom. They said it seemed as though a different set of rules operated in the classroom. If students did not understand the rules, they had difficulty participating in the learning routines of the classroom. One mother explained it to Heath (1982) in the following way:

> 'My kid, he too scared to talk, cause nobody play by the rules he know. At home I can't shut him up.' (p. 107)

Sometimes teachers interpret silence or nonparticipation by a student as disobedience, a lack of cooperation, or a lack of intelligence. It is possible that, like this woman's son, students simply do not know how to participate or are feeling inadequate.

Consider the implications of the research by Louden and Rivalland (1995) and Heath (1982) for the pedagogies of teachers' classrooms. Multiliterate students need to be able to operate in a range of contexts and understand social and cultural influences on literate practices. Therefore, teachers need to be aware of the literate practices in their classrooms. Teachers should think about how they conduct interactions and whether the routines of their classrooms are excluding some students.

Teachers also need to be aware of how their personal literacy identities influence the way they conduct school. For example, one teacher with whom the authors have worked said she came from a culture (Indian) that intrinsically valued education and schooling, and, therefore, she believed that it was a student's duty to participate in school and learn, even if the learning seemed irrelevant. She had not really been aware of how her cultural background was influencing her teaching until she started to examine her literacy identity and that of her students. A dedicated teacher, she was having difficulty motivating her students. Her students constantly asked her why they had to learn things, particularly in the area of math. Because of her background she considered this questioning as showing a lack of respect rather than as a genuine query. As she came to explore and compare her students' literacy identities with her own, she realised that she needed to modify her pedagogy to bring her understandings about schooling and those of her students closer together.

Therefore, she made a conscious effort to explain to students the relevance of what they were learning to their everyday lives and to investigate with them ways in which they might use the knowledge in different contexts. This meant that she gave up some control in the classroom, and the nature of their interactions became less formal and didactic. (In terms of the Productive Pedagogies previously discussed, they engaged in more substantive conversations.) The changes in this teacher's pedagogy increased the student participation and learning and reduced discipline problems over time.

However, because being multiliterate requires flexibility, being strategic, and coping with change, there is another very important element of the change that took place in this teacher's classroom pedagogy. She not only changed her pedagogy, but she also discussed with the students why she was changing it. She talked about how her literacy identity was influencing her teaching and then engaged the students in exploring and discussing how their literacy identities were influencing their learning. In this way her pedagogy not only developed the students' learning in terms of the subject-specific learning, such as math, but also in terms of understanding more about how literate practices operate in different settings and are influenced by culture. It further developed them as multiliterate citizens.

THEORY INTO PRACTICE: CLASSROOM APPLICATION

Exploring literacy identities with your students can help you and them understand the similarities and differences between school, classroom teacher, and student literate practices. The following ideas for this type of exploration have been developed by Leanne Moore of Weir State School in North Queensland, Australia. She used this information to reflect on the way her classroom operated as a social context and to develop appropriate and inclusive pedagogies. You may find that engaging in a similar lesson can help you to reflect and possibly change some of the pedagogy and routines of your classroom.

1. Introduce the concept of a literacy identity by modelling a way of recording your own literacy identity. Begin by discussing with the students that you are trying to map all the roles you have had in your life and the texts and literate practices you used when you engaged in those roles.

2. Ask the students to identify the best graphic organiser to map this information. For example, Leanne's class suggested an explosion map (see sample on page 66). They had previously done a lot of work on graphic organisers as a way of presenting or organising information, particularly focussing on how to identify the best organiser of the purpose and context.

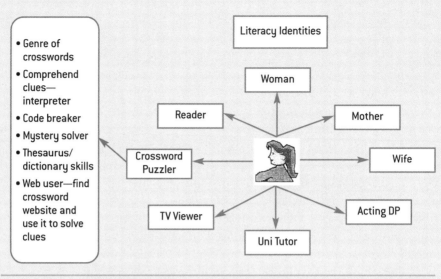

- Genre of crosswords
- Comprehend clues—interpreter
- Code breaker
- Mystery solver
- Thesaurus/dictionary skills
- Web user—find crossword website and use it to solve clues

Literacy Identities

Woman

Reader

Mother

Crossword Puzzler

Wife

TV Viewer

Acting DP

Uni Tutor

Source: Leanne Moore. Used with permission.

3. Model completing the roles section of your map and ask students to complete theirs. Then model completing the part of the map on texts and literate practices.

4. Lead a discussion concerning how they might use this information about themselves, focussing on the idea that a literacy identity is 'who I am as a text user'.

5. To revise the concept and check student learning, ask students to tell the teacher one of their literacy identities and give an example of the texts they would use and literate practices they would engage in as part of that identity. For example, in Leanne's class, one boy said that one of his literacy identities was a football player and that as a code breaker he had to know what the whistle meant. Another was a model maker; he had to operate as a code breaker and meaning maker to read and interpret diagrams and instructions.

Implicit Pedagogy

As noted previously, the classroom is a distinct social context that has particular routines and ways of interacting. It is essential for students to know and understand these routines if they are to learn successfully. One of the characteristics of the social environment of the classroom that has a significant effect on student learning is the way in which learning takes place through teacher–student interaction. A considerable body of research on this aspect of literacy pedagogy has been conducted and reported since the 1990s, examining how teacher–student interactions influence the types of knowledge conveyed and the way knowledge is constructed in the classroom (e.g., see Baker, 1991a, 1991b; Baker & Freebody, 1989a, 1989b; Edwards-Groves, 1999, 2003; Freebody, Ludwig, & Gunn, 1995; Freiberg & Freebody, 2001). Many of these studies conclude that the way talk, routines, and interactions around literacy learning occur sometimes prevents effective literacy learning from taking place. They suggest that literacy teaching is often too implicit and too random in focus.

In order to explain these conclusions we will examine the following interaction that is typical at the beginning of a lesson. (This is an hypothetical exchange based upon observations in classrooms.)

Teacher:	OK, let's talk about what we did after school yesterday. I went home, talked with a friend on the phone, took my kids to softball practice, cooked tea, and then I watched television. My favourite program was on [lists program]. What did you do, Caitlin?
Caitlin:	Dunno, nothing much.
Teacher:	Josh, what did you do?
Josh:	Um, I watched TV, I watched [lists three programs].

The students might think about the following questions as they listen to the teacher's initial statement. What was the purpose of this exchange; why did the teacher talk about what she did last night? What is this lesson going to be about? How am I expected to participate? What information should I supply? There are a number of possible answers. Perhaps the students have been learning about retelling or reporting information, and this question provides an opportunity to practice retelling events. Maybe they are going to discuss television programs and the teacher wants them to focus on what they watched, which is why that was the only part of her report that was elaborated. Possibly it is just a social conversation in which the teacher learns more about her students and builds rapport, or it could be a tactic she uses to settle them down before the actual lesson begins. In this case student participation is voluntary, and there is no assessment of responses in terms of ability to retell. Realistically the students can know what is really intended here only from past experience with the way this teacher and their classmates cooperate. There is no information provided; it is all implicit and random.

Rather than explicitly stating what learning is to take place and specifically demonstrating and talking about the literate practices to be discussed or taught, this interaction has simply engaged the students in literate practices and assumed they will know how to participate appropriately and work out what learning is taking place. The problem with such implicit teaching and engagement without explanation and focus is that although students may succeed with the task at that precise time, that success may be random and accidental. If so, they will not be able to draw conclusions from that engagement that will enable them to do the task again or transfer the learning to a slightly different situation. This approach does not encourage deep understanding about literacy and literate practices and the flexibility and strategic aspect of being multiliterate.

The research that has focussed on the implicit and social nature of classroom talk and student–teacher interactions suggests that because of the diverse cultural, social, and learning backgrounds of students, teachers need to be more explicit in the ways in which they conduct their pedagogy. Ludwig and Herschell (1998) investigated classroom talk and home talk. They concluded that there is a need for classroom talk to be more explicit in providing information about how to do literacy. These conclusions are not new; evidence indicating that explicit instruction might improve literacy has been reported by researchers working with students with specific reading difficulties for some time (e.g., see Bondy, 1984; Brown, 1985; Brown & Kane, 1988; Ellis, 1986; Paris, Cross, & Lipson, 1984). The concept of explicit instruction or explicit pedagogy in this context does not mean direct instruction. Rather it means conducting classroom talk and interaction that provides explicit information about literacy and literate practices. This can be achieved in many ways, through modelling and demonstration, direct teaching, guided investigation, substantive conversations, and discussion. It can be teacher or student directed, or jointly negotiated by students and teachers. The critical aspect is that the pedagogy and talk are explicit about what the purpose of the learning is and how it is to take place, and that they address both the knowledge about literacy and the how of literate practices.

THEORY INTO PRACTICE: CLASSROOM APPLICATION

An excellent way of reviewing the implicitness or explicitness of your pedagogy is to audiotape a part of your lessons. Audiotape the first 10 minutes of a few different lessons and listen to them. Listen to each lesson's beginning and answer the following questions:

1. Did you identify the learning purpose of the lesson for students?
2. Did you relate it to previous learning or lessons, or the current unit of work or theme so students had a context for this lesson?
3. Did you relate the learning to other contexts and discuss why it was useful to learn about this and how it might be used in the lifeworld as well as the school-based world?

4. Did you outline how the lesson would progress and what roles and responsibilities the students would have during the lesson?

5. Did you discuss or introduce any specialised terminology that might be used during the lesson?

Having reviewed the lesson beginnings, consider how you might change the beginning of future lessons in order to make them more explicit. This does not necessarily mean that you directly tell the students all the things identified in these five questions. This information can be derived from discussion, investigation, review of previous learning, or careful questioning. The important aspect is that students need to know why the discussion, investigation, review, or questioning is taking place.

For example, tell students, 'Over the last few weeks we have been looking at the life cycle of frogs in science. We have collected a lot of information and grouped it under headings, and today we need to develop a plan for how we can present this information to the students in year 2, who are only 7 years old. Let's start by thinking about what we already know about how to present information to a group from when we were studying the report genre a few weeks ago. Then, once we have identified what we know, we can use that knowledge to work out a plan of action for presenting information specifically about frogs to the year 2 group. By the end of this lesson I think we should have a plan. Now, what do we know about reports?'

Investigating Classroom Practice and How It Shapes Learning

There are three aspects to classroom practice (pedagogy) that are closely intertwined and influence the way in which learning takes place. These are

▸▸ classroom talk

▸▸ lesson structure

▸▸ materials used

Classroom Talk

The way in which talk is conducted in classrooms is unique to school settings. It mostly revolves around the exchange of questions and answers; that is, a teacher initiates a question, the students respond, and the teacher evaluates the answer, such as in the following example.

Teacher:	OK now, when we read the story of Little Red Riding Hood, one character was very bad. Who was that?
Student:	The Wolf.
Teacher:	Yes. The Wolf, that's right, good girl.

This pattern of exchange is often referred to as the IRF Model (initiate, respond, follow up), first researched by Sinclair and Coulthard (1975). Many researchers have continued to investigate the way in which these exchanges are conducted in classrooms and how that shapes learning.

French and MacLure (1981) explored how teachers assist students in obtaining the 'correct' answer during an IRF exchange. They found that often the exchange was not completed within three turns (initiation, response, follow-up). Frequently, after the initial question, a series of other exchanges occurred before the correct answer was given by a student and follow-up occurred. They found that sometimes teachers were so preoccupied with obtaining the one correct answer that they would reformulate questions in order to narrow the possible answers and obtain the correct one. Sometimes teachers would even give the answer in the form of a tag question, if all else failed. The following fictitious example and discussion of an extended IRF show how French and MacLure's research might be used to improve question-and-answer sequences in the classroom.

Teacher:	OK now, when we read the story of Little Red Riding Hood, one character was very bad. Who was that?
Student 1:	Little Red Riding Hood.
Teacher:	No, it wasn't Little Red Riding Hood. There was someone who did some really bad things.
Student 2:	Grandma.
Teacher:	No, it wasn't Grandma. Think about the story a little more.
Student 1:	The Woodcutter.
Teacher:	No, it was an animal who was very cruel.
Student 3:	The Wolf.
Teacher:	Yes, the Wolf was the bad character.

In this example, more and more hints have been given about the bad character so that students would arrive at the correct answer. Consider how useful these hints are to students if they ever have to identify a bad character in a narrative again (i.e., transfer these skills to another situation). They have been told that the character did some bad things, to think about the story a little more, and finally that it was a cruel animal. They have not been given any really useful or transferable information. These were simply clues to enable more accurate guesses about what was in the teacher's head. Consider the students' answers. Were any of them plausible? Little Red Riding Hood did indeed disobey her mother's instructions by talking to a stranger and wandering off the path to pick flowers. These could be construed as 'bad things'. But the students are not asked how they came to their answers so the teacher could give useful feedback.

How could this exchange be improved to provide students with learning that they could use again and in different ways? Here is an example, with alternatives and additions.

Original teacher question:	OK now, when we read the story of Little Red Riding Hood, one character was very bad. Who was that?
Alternative teacher comment:	We have been reading fairy tales, and one of the characteristics we have found is that there is often a bad character who has a major role in the story. Let's look at our most recent fairy tale and see what we can find out about bad characters and how we know they are bad.
Original student reply:	Little Red Riding Hood.
Alternative teacher response:	Well, that is not who I was thinking of, but tell me why you think Red Riding Hood was bad.
Possible student response:	She disobeyed her mother's instructions by talking to a stranger and wandering off the path to pick flowers.
Possible teacher response:	Well, you are quite right; you have justified that answer very well by using evidence from the story. You looked at what characters did to work out whether they were bad or not. However, Little Red Riding Hood only did bad things sometimes, so I don't think I would see her as the main bad character in the story, which is what we are talking about. Let's use your idea of looking for evidence and see if we can find a character who does mostly bad things in the story. Perhaps we could start a list of our characters and the things they did that were bad. This would help us.

In the revised exchange, the teacher has used the student's incorrect answer to further the students' understanding about bad characters. She has praised the student's logic and talked about the good strategies the student has used. She has then clarified what a bad character is (someone consistently doing the wrong thing) and suggested they build on the student's strategy to assemble evidence and find an answer. Another alternative would have been for the teacher to use guided questioning to get the students to come up with the strategy of listing all characters and their actions rather than suggesting it herself. Regardless, the revised exchange has provided information and strategies the students can use again in different settings. It has added to their repertoire of resources building multiliterate skills and knowledge.

The focus of this section has been on classroom talk. We suggest that analysing your classroom talk is extremely instructive, as it provides insights into exactly how you construct knowledge about literacy in your classroom. Because we are focussing on talk, we have suggested in the Theory Into Practice section on page 68 that you audiotape a lesson. Many people also videotape lessons, and this provides further information about body language, facial expression, the parts of the classroom, and particular children on whom you focus. We recommend this as a further way of examining your pedagogy. However, to begin with we suggest you audiotape and focus only on talk. A video will certainly record your talk. But you might find the visuals distracting, and it could be difficult to keep your focus on analysing the talk.

THEORY INTO PRACTICE: CLASSROOM APPLICATION

Try audiotaping some of your question-and-answer sequences, and evaluate the quality of your questioning in terms of teaching about literacy. The following questions might assist you when listening to the audiotape:

1. Do I preface the questioning with some information about why we are engaging in this discussion (the purpose of the learning)?

2. When I ask a question do I accept only the answer in my head or do I accept logical alternatives and discuss with students why they are logical alternatives?

3. What do I do with an incorrect answer? Do I ask the student how he or she arrived at that answer and then identify for the student where he or she went wrong? Or do I reject that answer and ask another student for an answer?

4. If I ask additional questions or give information to assist students in finding the answer, do I simply narrow the alternatives or do I actually provide information or strategies about how to get the answer?

Researchers have examined how the focus of exchanges in the classroom can influence the type of learning that takes place. Anstey (1998, 2003) found that talk had different functions in lessons, for example, management of behaviour, organisation, or provision of information. Anstey's study of 25 literacy lessons indicated that the exchanges of talk in the lessons gave students very little information about how to do the task or when the task might be useful. A high proportion of the talk was to do with management of the lesson rather than teaching about literacy. When students were engaged in literate practices the focus was on getting the task done rather than learning about how to do the task. Pedagogy often focussed on management and *doing* literacy (simply engaging in literate tasks) rather than *how* to do it and *why* learning about literacy and literate practices is useful. This approach does not foster the development of multiliteracies practices. This type of talk does not add to the student's repertoire of resources about literacy or provide opportunities to engage in and learn about flexible and strategic literate practices. Practising literate activity is very important, but so is understanding what you are doing, why you are doing it, and when it might be useful. Once again, teachers should seek balance.

Table 2 provides a set of categories and descriptors that Anstey developed about the relationship between the types of talk and the types of learning they encourage. In the centre column the focus or function of the talk or exchange is identified. The first two types of talk (classroom management and literacy information management) focus on management of behaviour or the literacy task at hand. These types of talk, although necessary to any classroom, do not teach about literacy; they simply facilitate the routines of the classroom. Consequently, teachers should keep these types of talk to a minimum. If teachers find that their lessons have a lot of this type of talk, they should consider why. To change that, they should think about how the class is organised and if routines can be streamlined.

TABLE 2
Functions of Teacher Talk

Talk Type/Definition (Clause Level)	Focus/Function (Exchange Level)	Example
1. Classroom Management • Questions and statements to do with the social and physical functioning of the classroom • Getting the group organised, discipline • No text focus • Questions and statements to do with previous non-literacy lessons	*Organisation* • Physical, social, and organisational management	• *Put your hands on your heads* • *Pens down* • *Turn around, Mandy* • *Right, OK* (continued)

TABLE 2 (continued)
Functions of Teacher Talk

Talk Type/Definition (Clause Level)	Focus/Function (Exchange Level)	Example
2. Literacy Information Management • Questions and statements to do with the function and procedures of a literacy lesson, unrelated to the literacy objectives of this lesson. They contain no relevant or implicit teaching of literacy, they simply facilitate the running of the literacy aspects of the lesson • May draw attention to the text but not as a meaning system • May recall, revise, give information from previous literacy lessons	• Management of literacy tasks • Doing the ritualised behaviour of school procedural display	• *Read the first page* • *Write in the first box* • *What can we see on the cover?* • *The author's name is...* • *Who illustrated this book?*
3. Reconstruction • Questions and statements which construct/reconstruct/paraphrase/rephrase the oral, written, or pictorial text of the lesson • Focus on behaviour with text rather than cognitive processes—doing the task rather than informing about the task • Doing literal or text-linking activities with the text	*Doing Literacy* • Implicit modelling/ teaching of task • Getting the task done	• *Alunak is excited because he is going on his first seal hunt* (paraphrasing the written text) • *I think I would write two main ideas here* (focus on doing the task, implicit modelling) • *Give me three reasons archaeology is interesting* (requiring recall of written text) • *Mary says that Alunak was Jim's friend* (rephrasing oral text of lesson, i.e. student's answer)
4. Elaboration/Projection • Questions and statements which model or require behaviour which involves use of knowledge beyond the text of the lesson, i.e., knowledge from students' life experience • Focus on doing the task rather than informing about the task	• Doing literacy rather than learning about how to do literacy	• *Who would we call on to provide good weather?* • *Well what is the order of merit?* • *What can you tell me about a Magpie?*
5. Informative • Questions and statements which give students information or definitions about the literacy skill/task/process but do not explain how to use this information to complete the task		• *Each paragraph has three main ideas* • *Usually the first sentence in the paragraph gives us the main idea*

(continued)

TABLE 2 (continued)
Functions of Teacher Talk

Talk Type/Definition (Clause Level)	Focus/Function (Exchange Level)	Example
6. Process • Questions or statements which explicitly explain the cognitive processes involved in the literacy task/process/skill which is the focus of the lesson	*Learning How, When, and Why About Literacy* • Cognition: how to do the task	• *What is better than guessing?* • *How would you work that out?* • *I am writing...because...*
7. Utility • Statements or questions which explain why the literacy skill/task/process which is the focus of the lesson is useful and how it might be useful in other situations	• Social practice: the utility of the skill/ process/task being learned	• *Why do we use paragraphs?* • *When we want to research a topic it is useful to look at the subheadings because they tell us where the information we want is located* • *That is a good answer because you are thinking about the use of that strategy* • *You skim because you need an idea of whether the information is good or not*

Source: Anstey, M. 'Examining Classrooms as Sites of Literate Practice and Literacy Learning'. In Anstey, M., & Bull, G. *The Literacy Lexicon* (2nd ed., p. 114). Pearson Education Australia, © 2004. Used with permission.

For example, some teachers provide an overview of tasks and materials needed for each session (morning, middle, or afternoon) on a designated display board, and students have to organise themselves for the whole session in the first 10 minutes after each break. Then the rest of the session is focussed more on learning than on organisation.

Another teacher uses a set of pigeonholes, one for each student. As students come into the room, they collect their materials, handouts, and texts for each session. Another class discusses appropriate behaviours for working individually or in groups. They have each behaviour written on a card and hung on strings around the room at pupil height. They routinely monitor each other's behaviour. If they observe inappropriate behaviour, they draw one another's attention to the problem quietly by pointing to the relevant behaviour card. Alternatively, they simply remove themselves from the situation and isolate the person behaving badly. This routine has taken only three to four weeks to establish in a very difficult classroom and has had enormous impact on the classroom interactions. As a result, the class focusses much more on learning than on behaviour management.

The next three types of talk listed in Table 2 (reconstruction, elaboration or projection, and informative) focus learning on doing literacy. These types of exchanges implicitly teach by engaging in the task but do not focus on how its is being done and why it is useful. A good example of this is the earlier Red Riding Hood exchange. In that case, the teacher repeated students' incorrect answers and told them they were incorrect but offered no additional help (re-construction talk). Sometimes a teacher needs to repeat or paraphrase an answer because students cannot hear it or the teacher wants to emphasise it, but simply repeating it is not useful. The elaboration talk can exclude some students if they do not have the general knowledge to draw on in order to participate or answer. However, if used appropriately this type of talk can show students how they use their literacy identities and all the resources they have to assist them in literate practices. Again, the key is how this talk is used and how often. Similarly, informative talk that provides definitions and terminology is essential, but a definition or a term is useless if the student does not know how and when to use it. The teacher should strive for balance.

The final two categories, process and utility, are the most important in achieving classroom talk and exchanges that contribute to a multiliteracies pedagogy. These types of talk should be highly visible in lessons, because they explore the how and why of literate practices and provide the deep learning and understandings that enable transformation of knowledge.

THEORY INTO PRACTICE: CLASSROOM APPLICATION

Try audiotaping and analysing some of your lessons in terms of the types of talk or exchanges you use and how they are distributed across your lesson. Ideally you would transcribe your lesson, as the written record allows a more accurate and in-depth examination of your talk. Many teachers have found this in-depth analysis of a lesson to be a turning point in their teaching.

Typically, you will transcribe one lesson of about 30 minutes. Write each speaking turn by a student or teacher on a new line. Then use the seven categories in Table 2 to classify the talk. You might want to use seven different colours of highlighter pens, one for each type of talk. Highlight the talk on the transcript in terms of its type. For example, all classroom management talk might be highlighted in yellow. A good question to ask yourself when trying to classify your talk is 'What did the students learn from this talk?'

The advantage of the coloured transcript is you can immediately see what your talk focusses on and then evaluate whether it is appropriate or not. If you find that there is a lot of informative talk, that is not necessarily a bad thing. It might have been appropriate for that lesson or that part of the lesson. It depends on the learning focus.

After listening to yourself and doing some analysis of the transcript, you might want to consider taking some action to make your talk more focussed on multiliterate behaviour. Try to focus on one aspect at a time. For example, try to use less management talk, or try to concentrate on the how and why of literate tasks rather than just doing them.

The following questions might assist you when listening to the audiotape:

1. What is the major focus of talk in the lesson?

2. If the focus is on management, what was it that made this so (e.g., behaviour, lack of familiarity with the activity or strategy used)?

3. How can I manage and plan my lessons to reduce management talk?

4. How can I provide more information about how to do the task and when it is useful?

5. Can I engage students in a real-life example to assist in the learning and thus demonstrate its utility?

6. Did I model thinking as well as behavioural aspects of the literate task when I explained how to do the task?

Lesson Structure

The exchanges, interaction, and talk in a lesson are focussed in different ways at different points in the lesson. For example, at the beginning of a lesson when students are being oriented to an activity, there may be more organisational talk. Then as the learning focus of the lesson is identified, you would expect more informative and utility talk as the concept is identified and the usefulness of learning about it is discussed. If modelling is taking place there should be a lot of informative and procedural talk, and the intellectual (cognitive) and social behaviours should be modelled and discussed. This link between the stage of the lesson and the talk that would be most useful at that point is a critical one. The implication is that teachers need to be very strategic about how they plan a lesson. They need to think about not only what will be done and learned, but how it will be talked about and what is the most appropriate sequence and structure for doing it. Therefore, teachers should think about the structure of the lesson and understand how it can influence learning.

Learning episodes or lessons proceed through a sequence of activities. For example, the lesson might begin with the teacher discussing various examples of a genre with the students in order to identify its characteristics. The students might then be asked to move into groups, and to collaboratively identify and label the characteristics of that genre on a large print example of the genre. The groups would then nominate one person to report their findings to the class. The lesson would conclude with the teacher and students jointly constructing a list of the characteristics of the genre and labelling another example for a poster reference to be displayed in the room.

Each of these activities can be termed a phase in the lesson, and each phase requires particular types of oral interaction, social behaviour, and intellectual or cognitive activity. Each time students move to a new phase of the lesson (e.g., from discussing the example with the teacher to collaboratively labelling in a group, to individually presenting a report on that activity), they are required to behave and interact slightly differently. Therefore, in order to participate successfully in a lesson and learn, students need to be able to recognise the phase structures, know how to behave within them, and identify when transition occurs from one phase to the next.

Similarly teachers need to consider the phase structure of their lessons, ensuring that the phases and activities within them are the most appropriate for the learning purpose. The phases should follow a logical sequence, and the teacher should make the learning purposes of each phase and the connections between them clear through his or her talk to students. For example, at the beginning of the lesson, it would be useful to outline the learning purpose, the sequence of activities to be undertaken, and how each activity will contribute to the learning purpose (e.g., 'We have looked at the characteristics of this genre together in a number of examples. Now we are going to try to apply this knowledge to another example in small groups. This will enable you to review how well you have understood this and practice applying your new knowledge.'). In this way students are able to prepare for their learning and think about how they should behave and interact at each stage. They will also be able to activate the resources and prior knowledge that they have to help them with each phase. This will encourage the flexible and strategic nature of being multiliterate as well as transformation.

Anstey (1998, 2003) investigated the phase structure of lessons and developed categories and definitions for analysing and identifying the structure of lessons. Anstey found that some phases are essential to the successful lesson structure. They may not all occur in one lesson, and they may not occur in the order presented here. But overall the following phases are essential to the deep learning and understanding of concepts:

- *focus*—identifying the learning purpose and its relevance to school-based world and lifeworld activities, and outlining how the lesson will progress
- *identifying*—recognising new concepts when they are defined, explored, modelled, or discussed; guided or unguided by the teacher, depending on whether the concept is new, a revision, or an extension of knowledge
- *practice*—practicing application of the concept in similar contexts, for similar purposes

- *transfer*—using the concept in new ways for different purposes in different contexts and combining it with other knowledge; encouraging transformation
- *review*—reviewing the learning purpose of the whole lesson or the particular phase and its relevance and usefulness; may occur several times in a lesson but absolutely essential at the end
- *report*—reviewing what the students know and understand by asking them to self-monitor and report

It is important to remember the connection between lesson structure and talk. A lesson may have a very logical and carefully sequenced structure, and all the activities the students engage in might be highly relevant. However, if the talk in the lesson does not support this structure, then the learning will be dissipated. It is also important to consider how many phases are appropriate to the lesson, that is, how often will students change tasks and behaviours. If there are too many changes the students may become confused about the focus of the lesson. In addition, the many changes in behaviour and patterns of interaction that come with the phase changes may intrude on the learning.

Materials

When thinking about the phases of the lesson, the focus inevitably turns to the materials to be used. This is the appropriate time to consider materials. In other words when planning a lesson the sequence of general questions should be

1. What is the desired learning outcome? What do I want my students to know and be able to do at the end of this lesson?
2. How might I structure this lesson?
3. What sorts of talk will facilitate the type of learning I want to achieve in each phase?
4. What are the best materials to facilitate this lesson?

Although it is tempting to start with the last question, there is a danger that selecting the materials first may have a detrimental effect on the talk and lesson structure. Teachers should select and use materials strategically to enhance the type of learning that is to take place in that phase of the lesson, and the materials should facilitate the type of talk that is best used in that phase. For example, a teacher might select a commercially produced blackline master to teach about inferential comprehension skills. The teacher might use this for the identifying phase of the lesson, carefully working through it with the students. The danger here is that the teacher's talk might become focussed more on literacy management and reconstruction (doing the task or worksheet) rather than on procedural and utility-type information (learning how and why) about inferential comprehension. The blackline master or worksheet might be useful for practice or maybe even transformation if it is a high-quality worksheet, and that is the phase it should be used in.

The same decisions need to be made about using new technological aids such as whiteboards that connect to a printer, computers, digital projectors, and screens. Teachers are sometimes tempted to think that they cannot teach without all the latest technology, particularly when teaching about new technologies. However, if a teacher is asking students to write a report and present it using PowerPoint, students will have a lot of work to do before they need to use the computer. Certainly they need to know about PowerPoint and its capabilities, but the teacher can demonstrate this using a laptop and a digital projector. Then the students can do the planning and storyboards for their presentations, organising the written, visual, and oral content. Having done all this planning, then they can learn to use the software and put the PowerPoint presentation together. In this way the focus becomes planning reports and presenting to an audience using electronic texts, rather than learning how to use PowerPoint software. The software package might be obsolete in a year or two, but the knowledge about planning a presentation using an electronic text and the linguistic, auditory, and visual semiotic systems will not. Students will be able to use these resources in many contexts for many purposes in years to come. This is what a multiliteracies pedagogy aims to do.

Summary: Characteristics of Dynamic Pedagogy

This chapter has examined the general principles of a multiliteracies curriculum and the characteristics of a multiliteracies pedagogy. This journey has covered the general principle of a productive pedagogy and the need to teach explicitly rather than implicitly. Examples have shown how to look at the minutiae of the lesson; the minute to minute unfolding of the talk, lesson structure, and materials; and the relationships between them.

To bring it all together, teachers should strive for the characteristics of a dynamic pedagogy that develops a multiliterate, active, and informed citizen. A dynamic pedagogy

- ◗◗ is functional and goal directed, with the functions and goals explicitly stated;
- ◗◗ is made relevant to students by explicitly showing and exploring links to their school-based world and lifeworld;
- ◗◗ develops and enhances concepts about literacy and literate practices as well as skills, that is, deep learning and understanding;

- contains explanations and demonstrations that provide students with a metalanguage for talking about literacy;

- encourages students to self-monitor their learning and apply it in different ways with other resources that they have at their disposal;

- acknowledges students' individual literacy identities, the social and cultural and technological characteristics of their community in the selection of content and teaching strategies, and the conduct of classroom routines and interactions;

- incorporates opportunities to consume, practice, apply, and transform learning; and

- uses materials that are best suited to the learning outcome and that resemble or are a part of life outside the classroom.

A dynamic multiliteracies pedagogy is concerned with making decisions about learning that are based on the relationships between the desired learning outcomes, what teachers know about their students, and what teachers know about the way in which successful pedagogy is conducted. This relationship is shown in Figure 7. Making informed decisions about how to approach the teaching of particular learning outcomes, together with reviewing and reflecting on pedagogy in focussed ways, should ensure a dynamic pedagogy that continues to evolve as the knowledge about pedagogy increases and the demands of literacy change.

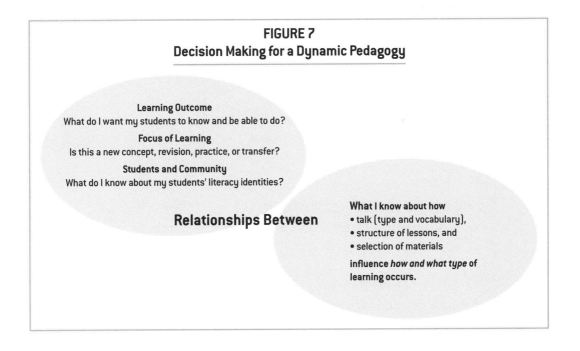

FIGURE 7
Decision Making for a Dynamic Pedagogy

Learning Outcome
What do I want my students to know and be able to do?

Focus of Learning
Is this a new concept, revision, practice, or transfer?

Students and Community
What do I know about my students' literacy identities?

Relationships Between

What I know about how
- talk (type and vocabulary),
- structure of lessons, and
- selection of materials

influence *how and what type* of learning occurs.

CHAPTER 4

The New Literacies and Children's Literature

This chapter examines the field of children's literature from the point of view that it represents traditional print texts and also visual texts. Children's literature itself is a product of the changing times and therefore an excellent place for teachers to commence a study of new literacies and to engage in multiliteracies.

As discussed earlier, changing literacies are linked to changing times, which are characterised by ever-increasing change in the workplace and technology, and by increasing social and cultural diversity. The new literacies and, particularly, multiliteracies provide grounds for redefining the traditional approaches and ideologies in literacy. With the advent of multiliteracies has come a need to revisit the whole question of pedagogy and how changes in the way teachers view literacy has produced a concomitant change in the pedagogy of literacy.

Text can no longer be seen as print only amid a much more visual culture with the increased use of images in information and communication technologies. These visual texts require new ways of understanding and new systems of analysis for the full realisation of meaning by the reader and viewer. This is not to suggest that preexisting texts are irrelevant and to be consigned to some forgotten place in the history of literacy. What it does suggest is that the study of how these new texts are constructed and reconstructed is an important part of the change in literacy pedagogy. There is also a need to look at different ways of constructing meaning and producing new readings in texts that were written before the advent of these new literacies.

Children's Literature: The Picture Book

Picture books have been a recognisable genre in children's literature for hundreds of years. In 1484 William Caxton printed *Aesop's Fables*, the first book to be printed on a printing press. Although it was not initially seen as a book for children, it quickly became a perennial favourite. The first book written especially for young readers was the *Orbis Pictus* in 1658. Both these books contained words and pictures and can be seen as the forerunners of the modern picture book. Interestingly, in the five centuries since, much effort has been directed towards teaching about reading the words—but rarely about reading the pictures. This seems all the more ironic because *Orbis Pictus* literally showed young readers 'around the world in pictures' and was a type of encyclopaedia with illustrations. Furthermore, *Aesop's Fables* was illustrated throughout with woodcuts. This focus on illustration highlights the case for a reconsideration of the treatment of the modern picture book. In these new times, teachers and students will benefit from concentrating on both the visual and print text. Picture books are not necessarily part of the 'old literacy', but students can benefit from finding new ways of reading them. Picture books, comprising traditional print and visual literacies, provide students with opportunities to practice new literacies.

As readers read and engage with text in new ways, the literacy agenda for the 21st century should encompass the following understandings about text:

1. All texts are consciously constructed and have particular social, cultural, political, and economic purposes.

2. Text comes in a variety of representational forms incorporating a range of grammar rules and semiotic systems.

3. The reader or viewer may need to draw on several sets of grammar rules and semiotic systems in order to engage with some texts.

4. Changes in society and technology will continue to challenge and affect texts and their representational forms.

5. There may be more than one way of reading or viewing a text depending on a range of contextual (e.g., social, cultural, economic, or political) factors.

6. There is a need to consider the possible meanings of a text and how it is constructing the reader and the world of the reader.

Teachers will need to look at text in new ways to help students acquire these understandings and to empower students to participate fully in global economies. The picture book of the 20th and 21st centuries is itself a product of changing times (Bull & Anstey, 2004). The contemporary picture book incorporates characteristics that require these six understandings on the part of the reader and therefore is particularly suited to the teaching of new literacies. This type of picture book has been commonly referred to as a postmodern picture book since the close of the 20th century (Arizpe & Styles, 2003; Grieve, 1993; Lewis, 1990; Watson & Styles, 1996). The narrative in a postmodern picture book is constructed by the illustrative text through the images and by the written text through the words. In order to engage with such a book, an individual needs to be both a reader and a viewer—that is, to be a reader of pictures as well as a reader of words. This requires the reader to be knowledgeable not only about how the grammar of written text assists in the construction of meaning, but also about how the grammar of illustrative text constructs meaning. Thus a postmodern picture book has multiple meanings, and sometimes these are contesting discourses in which the narrative in the illustrative text is contrary, rather than complementary, to the meaning in the written text. Other meanings are often created by using different narrators or different points of view that require the reader and viewer to take a different perspective, using an indeterminate ending that requires the reader and viewer to supply the ending, or using intertextuality, requiring the reader and viewer to access other picture books that contain the same meanings.

Contesting discourses, different narrators and points of view, and intertextuality are examples of literary devices that authors and illustrators employ to construct a postmodern picture book. Waugh (1984) calls them metafictive devices because they are consciously or purposefully used by the author or illustrator to construct the narrative in a particular way. This in turn makes new or alternative meanings available to the reader and viewer. Metafictive devices act in the same way as metacognitive strategies to help people understand how they know they are completing their tasks. Because many, but not all, contemporary authors and illustrators are consciously employing particular devices to affect the way an individual reader and viewer interacts with a narrative, the ultimate success of the act of reading a postmodern picture book depends on an individual's knowledge of those devices. The use of the devices is a literary choice that the author and illustrator make, expecting the reader and viewer to be aware of the new literacies required to fully engage with the narrative.

Sometimes what we have termed a metafictive device can be used by authors and illustrators simply because, through experience, they have come to know that a particular technique is successful. In this way it is not a conscious choice made purposefully for a particular reason. In the four picture books discussed in the following Reflection Strategy, all have employed a metafictive device. In Maurice Sendak's *Where the Wild Things Are* (1963) and John Burningham's *Come Away From the Water, Shirley* (1977), the authors may or may not have known about, or consciously employed, a particular device. Given the time when the books were written, however, they most likely were unaware of them. Still, knowledge of such devices by a reader and viewer potentially enhances the meanings available, irrespective of the intensions of the author and illustrator. On the other hand, author Allan Baillie and illustrator Jane Tanner in *Drac and the Gremlin* (1988) and author Gary Crew and illustrator Steven Woolman in *Tagged* (1997a) have indicated through discussions that the use of metafictive devices was intentional.

1. Choose a picture book such as *Where the Wild Things Are* by Maurice Sendak (1963) or *Come Away From the Water, Shirley* by John Burningham (1977) and look at the way the meanings in the written text differ from those in the illustrative text. (If these books are unavailable then you may wish to consult the list of postmodern picture books in the Further Reading section at the end of this book, pages 141–142). Sendak refers to the gnashing and roaring of the wild things in the written text, whereas in the illustrative text the wild things are always smiling. This is a good example of contesting discourses and is perhaps why, when the book was first published, many parents thought it was frightening and yet young children were delighted by it. The parent audience was attending to the written text while the young children were 'reading' the pictures.

   Burningham incorporates two illustrative texts in his picture book, one supporting the narrative involving the parents of Shirley on the beach, and the second showing the imaginative adventures that Shirley is undertaking. These two illustrative texts are shown on opposing pages right through the book so that the reader and viewer is constantly meeting the two different meanings that are being constructed by the images. The written text accompanying the illustrations assists in interpreting the parents' actions and demonstrates how the meanings created from the parents' and Shirley's viewpoints differ.

2. As you are studying the books consider the following questions:

   • What are the metafictive devices present in the book? How are they used?

   • What effect do these devices have on the narrative?

   • Is the book more interesting because of the presence of the devices? How and why?

   • Would young readers be able to understand, and then use, these devices?

3. Look at the two illustrations on pages 86 and 87 and carry out the same analysis as before, using the four questions as a guide. In *Drac and the Gremlin* (1988), by author Allan Baillie and illustrator Jane Tanner, the narrative is a simple story of two children playing in their backyard and constructing a game of make-believe. Interestingly, although we use the

terms *author* and *illustrator*, in postmodern picture books the narrative is constructed as much by the images as it is by the words. It may be more accurate to think of Baillie as author of the words and Tanner as author of the images. Seldom is the illustrator given as much recognition as the author in the construction of the narrative, and typically illustrators are not mentioned in references listings.

Illustration and Written Text From *Drac and the Gremlin*

Drac and the Gremlin leap aboard her Anti-Gravity Solar-Powered Planet Hopper. They sweep through the clouds to the mountain of the White Wizard.

Source: Baillie, A. *Drac and the Gremlin* (J. Tanner, Ill.). Pearson Group Australia, © 1998. Used with permission.

This is a good example of contesting discourses, in which the expectation built up by the words differs markedly from the meanings suggested by the images associated with the words. At this point in the narrative, young readers and viewers tend to fully understand how Baillie and Tanner are playing with them, and their response is one of pure delight. Five-year-old students in their first year of school not only have been able to understand the differences between the written and illustrative texts but they also can infer reasons why the texts are different.

4. *Tagged* (1997a), written by Gary Crew and illustrated by Steven Woolman, is a postmodern picture book designed for older students who are 10 to 12 years old. It tells the story of a Vietnam veteran who is talking to a teenage

boy about his experiences during the war as an Australian soldier. During the narrative it becomes apparent that the veteran has been seriously affected—tagged—by his experiences.

Illustration and Written Text From *Tagged*

Source: Crew, G. *Tagged* (S. Woolman, Ill.). Era Publications, Australia, © 1997. Used with permission.

Both the illustrative and written texts draw heavily on other texts to realise their full meaning. Intertextuality is used here as a metafictive device. It is important to realise that the other texts that *Tagged* draws on are not only print texts. The still and moving images that many older people associate with the Vietnam war are also texts, and they play an important part in the construction of the different meanings to be found in this narrative.

5. You may wish to choose books from the list of picture books in the Additional Children's Literature Resources on pages 143–144 to explore the use of other metafictive devices in postmodern picture books.

6. Consider your understandings of the points below:

- How are postmodern picture books constructed?

- What techniques do the author and illustrator employ to construct different meanings in the text?

- What common metafictive devices are used in postmodern picture books?

THEORY INTO PRACTICE: CLASSROOM APPLICATION

Once you have an understanding of what makes a picture book postmodern and have an appreciation of the metafictive devices that are used in them, try the following ideas in the classroom.

Activity 1

If you have access to John Burningham's *Come Away From the Water, Shirley* (1977) or the sequel *Time to Get Out of the Bath, Shirley* (1978), these can be used with students of any age. The books use two illustrative texts, only one of which agrees with the written text. These all appear on each double-page spread, so it is easy to show the class how the narrative is unfolding. Although this book is designed for young readers, given the learning focus of this task, it is reasonable to use the book with older readers. However, you must first explain the learning purpose so students do not feel they are using a so-called baby book. After this activity, you could ask students to identify other books they have come across that have some of these metafictive devices.

1. Ask the class why there are two different illustrations for each line of written text. Most students readily understand that one set of illustrations represents an imaginary adventure that Shirley is having. They should also be able to provide justifiable reasons for her pretending—for example, because her parents are having a quiet (boring) time. They might justify this reason by pointing to the bright colours on Shirley's pages and the black-and-white images on the parents' pages. Bright colours indicate action and excitement, and black and white symbolise boredom and lack of action.

2. The point of this questioning sequence and the discussion that it promotes is for students to realise the role that the illustrative text plays in the construction of meaning—in this case multiple meanings. There is another important lesson here that is also a feature of postmodern picture books; that is, a narrative does not have just one meaning. This is an important point for you as a teacher to make; otherwise, your students might always look to you for *the* meaning of the text. If this meaning is not forthcoming, students might engage in guessing what is inside the teacher's head. This will not help them to find the meanings in a narrative, because guessing is not a suitable strategy for developing comprehension ability.

Activity 2

1. Find two versions of the same narrative. (This activity is suitable for younger and older students, but students will bring different levels of understanding and sophistication about text to the activity. That is, they will discover different things.) This is very easy with fairy tales, because

there are many different versions of these stories available. For example, compare different versions of the Frog Prince tale such as *The Frog Prince* (1990) by Jan Ormerod or *The Frog Princess?* (1995), written by Pamela Mann and illustrated by Jill Newton, which is told from the frog's point of view. An even more challenging version of the Frog Prince is the continuation, or sequel, entitled *The Frog Prince Continued* (1991), written by Jon Scieszka and illustrated by Steve Johnson. It is an excellent way of exploring different points of view, because the sequel is written from the prince's point of view rather than from the princess's. The important point here is not *which versions* you use but that you use *different versions* of the same tale. There are many versions available of Cinderella, Little Red Riding Hood, the Selfish Giant, Noah stories, and so on. (Examples of multiple versions of some of these books are provided in the Additional Children's Literature Resources on page 144.)

2. Use the following guiding questions to focus on the differences among the different versions:

   ‣ Who is telling the story?

   ‣ How is the story in version one different from the story in version two or three?

   ‣ What difference does this make?

   ‣ Why have the authors written different stories in the two or more versions?

   ‣ Why have the illustrators drawn different illustrations in the two or more versions?

   ‣ How are the illustrations in version one different from the illustrations in version two or three?

   ‣ What difference does this make?

3. You may need to make the discussions more specific in later lessons or activities by making comments such as the following:

   ‣ 'Let's look at how the characters (or setting, moral, theme) are different in each version.'

   ‣ 'Today we are going to focus on the use of colour (or line, format, vectors) in each version.' (For more information about analysing the illustrative text see chapter 5.)

   ‣ 'We are going to talk today about what point of view means. First of all we are going to look at what difference it makes when the illustrator draws a scene from a different direction. Illustrators have different points of view just as authors do. Later we will look at the author's point of view.' (Students tend to find it easy to understand point of view from the illustrator's perspective. They can then go on to discuss the author's point of view. If the author's point of view is introduced first, then this tends to cause difficulty for some students.)

Postmodern Picture Book as a Text for Changing Times

The postmodern picture book, by its very construction, uses particular metafictive elements to interrupt reader expectation and to produce multiple readings and meanings (Grieve, 1993). Authors and illustrators have begun to self-consciously construct text, encompassing print and visual elements to create diverse and divergent meanings, challenging the traditional audiences, and questioning established plots, characters, and even settings. The result is a blend of illustrative and fictive styles that produce picture books that look quite different and are to be read quite differently. In the postmodern picture book, because both the author and illustrator are involved in the construction of meaning, there is potential to create a range of different meanings. The postmodern picture book has become an ideal setting for agreements and contradictions to occur between written and illustrative text and for contesting discourses to be set up. With these developments has come a reconsideration of audience; the contemporary picture book is no longer seen as primarily for young readers. The postmodern devices that are now often incorporated into picture books make them relevant and appealing to older age groups with higher reading abilities and more sophisticated interests. As described in Anstey and Bull (2000) and Anstey (2002a), the devices commonly employed include the following:

- Nontraditional ways of using plot, character, and setting challenge reader and viewer expectations and require different ways of reading and viewing. For example, in *The Frog Prince Continued* (Scieszka, 1991), the princess nags and is unattractive. The continuation indicates that not all fairy tales have happy endings.

- Unusual uses of the narrator's voice position the reader and viewer to read the book in particular ways and through particular characters' eyes (this can be achieved by the written or visual text). For example, in *Come Away From the Water, Shirley* (Burningham, 1977), there are two narratives. One is told through the parents' instructions to Shirley, and the other is told entirely through the illustrations on the facing page, which depict a pirate adventure Shirley is imagining.

- Indeterminacy in written or illustrative text, plot, character, or setting requires the reader to construct some of the text and meanings. For example in *The Viewer* (1997b), written by Gary Crew and illustrated by Shaun Tan, the reader is left to work out what has happened to the main character.

▸▸ A pastiche of illustrative styles requires the reader and viewer to employ a range of knowledge and grammar rules to read. For example, in *The Rabbits* (1998), written by John Marsden and illustrated by Shaun Tan, almost every page uses a different style of illustration. In *Sand Swimmers* (1999), written and illustrated by Narelle Oliver, a different illustrative technique is used for different types of information in the book. This provides a code to tell the reader which illustrations support which parts of the text.

▸▸ Changes to traditional book formats, with new and unusual designs and layouts, challenge the reader's and viewer's perceptions about how to read a book. For example, in *Black and White* (1990), written and illustrated by David Macaulay, each spread is divided into four quadrants. Each quadrant is illustrated in a particular style and medium and tells a different but connected story. The reader is left to work out the connections.

▸▸ Contesting discourses (between illustrative and written text) require the reader to consider alternate readings and meaning. Examples of this have previously been given (e.g., *Come Away From the Water, Shirley*, Burningham, 1977).

▸▸ Intertextuality requires the reader and viewer to access and use background knowledge from other texts in order to access the available meanings. An example of this is *The Jolly Postman: Or Other People's Letters* (1986) by Janet and Allan Ahlberg, which contains actual letters related to different fairy tales. The reader is left to make the link from the mail to the fairy tale.

▸▸ The availability of multiple readings and meanings for a variety of audiences. A good example of this is *The Ghost Dance* (1995), written by Alice McLerran and illustrated by Paul Morin, in which there are many possible readings. It may be about the coming of the white man, about pollution, and about the strength of people's culture in the face of adversity. *The Rabbits* (Marsden, 1998), mentioned previously, is an Australian book with similar multiple themes. *The Rabbits* might be an interesting book to compare and contrast with *The Ghost Dance*.

Although metafictive devices are more apparent in recently published picture books, there is evidence of them in some well-known earlier publications. For example, in *Where the Wild Things Are* (1963), Maurice Sendak deliberately subverted many of the established rules about character, language, and illustration by creating a main character who was angry and disobedient, by constructing sentences that ranged over five pages, and by producing illustrations that constantly changed size. While Sendak's avowed purpose was to incorporate fantasy into the narrative, the text can be read differently from a postmodern perspective. The text resists a single reading or meaning very successfully, creating a range of alternative readings. Certainly when it was first published children read it differently from adults, with interpretations varying from a fun-filled fantasy to a frightening nightmare. Sendak went on, particularly in *Outside Over There* (1981) and *Dear Mili* (1988), to use a pastiche of illustrative texts that relied on constant intertextual references by the viewer and a sophisticated background knowledge of art history.

Similarly, early picture books in Britain and Australia also exhibited what we would now term postmodern characteristics. In Australia, Jenny Wagner incorporated intertextual references in the title of the book *John Brown, Rose and the Midnight Cat* (1977). The use of the name 'John Brown' draws attention to the role that the dog John Brown has in protecting his mistress, like the servant John Brown who protected Queen Victoria. Not all readers will be able to make all the connections that could be taken up by more sophisticated audiences. However, readers—even as young as 5 or 6—are often more capable than expected (see Arizpe & Styles, 2003; Doonan, 1993). Although access to metafictive devices is usually not necessary to fully understand or enjoy a book, such awareness can make further readings and meanings available to the reader and viewer. Picture books also can be used to investigate issues related to culture and history (see Anstey & Bull, 2000). Table 3 outlines these connections as well as how written and illustrative texts can be used to create alternative readings and meanings.

Postmodern Picture Books as a Way of Investigating New Times and New Literacies

As we have discussed, present-day authors and illustrators have a variety of metafictive devices available to them if they wish to encourage multiple readings and create possibilities for alternative meanings. The British author and illustrator Anthony Browne has often been reported in interviews (see Evans, 1998) as utilising intertextuality by incorporating particular images (the art work of Magritte in *Willy the Dreamer*, Browne, 1997) or recurring characters (such as gorillas) to promote different readings. In Australia, Shaun Tan (see Bull, 1998) reported deliberately using a pastiche of illustrative styles in *The Rabbits* (Marsden, 1998) to cultivate the creation of different meanings by the viewer. The American author and illustrator David Macaulay in *Black and White* (1990) issued a warning on the title page that the following book might contain a number of stories or perhaps just one. In order to deal with this contradiction the reader and viewer is advised to inspect the words and pictures.

TABLE 3
Creating Alternative Meanings Through Illustrative and Written Texts in Picture Books

Picture Book	Written Text Use	Illustrative Text Use
Wojciechowski, S., & Lynch, P.J. (1995). *The Christmas Miracle of Jonathan Toomey*. Walker Books, London.	• A study of the celebration of Christmas • Early American village life—buildings, dress, and customs • Exploration of loneliness and companionship	• Study of literal illustration (photorealism) • Character development through illustration—body position, facial expression • Conveying emotion—light, body position, facial expression
Wisniewski, D. (1996). *Golem*. Clarion Books, New York.	• Jewish ghetto in Poland • Supernatural versus religious belief • Value of life and death • Limits of human power	• Study of media: cut paper illustration • Use of light and dark colour for mood • Balance and lack of balance to denote chaos
Steptoe, J. (1987). *Mufaro's Beautiful Daughters*. Lothrop, Lee & Shepard Books, New York.	• Life in Zimbabwe • African village life—dress, customs, flora and fauna • Caring for others brings rewards, selfishness is punished • Male and female roles	• Construction of characters—colour of clothes, body decoration, body position (angular/angry, rounded/demure), position of arms, direction of eyes
Burningham, J. (1999). *Whadayamean*. Jonathan Cape, London.	• Anti war • Study of effects of pollution • Religious intolerance • Irony—children's 'dream' • Intertextual references here to *Mr Gumpy's Outing* (characters and boat), which is also about cooperation	• Different media—photographs and collage—why? • Why is Middle East shown on picture of Earth? • Use of 'real' text—newspaper • Body position and gesture to show emotions
McCully, E.A. (1992). *Mirette on the High Wire*. Ashton Scholastic, Sydney.	• Study of 18th-century Paris • Lives of painters—Renoir, Toulouse-Lautrec • Explore the notion of fear and courage	• Style and period is reminiscent of Impressionists: study the different styles of Renoir and Lautrec • Use of colour and light—brown tones for Bellini and white and red for Mirette • Use of pastel
Oliver, N. (1999). *Sand Swimmers*. Lothian, Melbourne.	• Analyse the structure and purpose of faction [a mixture of fiction and fact] genre • Layers of histories of Australia, the explorers, discovery of Australia • The different beauty of central Australia	• Study of media and styles and how they are used to show the different histories and types of information
Thompson, C., & Pignataro, A. (1998). *The Staircase Cat*. Hodder, Melbourne.	• Study of war, particularly World War II • Look at anti-war movements • Cycles of life and renewal	• Look at layout—off balance, odd angles, placement of elements in pictures • Balance returns with peace • Use of changes in colour • Body postures change in war and in peace

(continued)

TABLE 3 (continued)
Creating Alternative Meanings Through Illustrative and Written Texts in Picture Books

Picture Book	Written Text Use	Illustrative Text Use
Crew, G., & Tan, S. (1999). *Memorial*. Lothian, Melbourne.	• Investigate the topic of memories—intergenerational family and memory of wars • Futility of war • Discussion of the idea that memories outlast memorials	• Use of different media, design, and layout to illustrate simultaneous representations of the past/present • Use of wordless double spreads • Use of symbolism rather than literal illustrative text • Discuss reasons for above
Marsden, J., & Tan, S. (1998). *The Rabbits*. Lothian, Melbourne.	• Study of different invasions (e.g. alien, white invasion of Australia, colonial) • Loss of power and self • Discussion of environmental messages • The lost generations	• Study of the styles of Arthur Boyd and the Surrealists • Investigate why the rabbits are not depicted literally • Why do the Australian animals mutate? • Many of the scenes are similar to images in SF magazines. Why? • Use of colour to reflect mood
Norman, L., & Young, N. (1998). *Grandpa*. Margaret Hamilton, Sydney.	• Relationships between different generations in a family • Discussions about life and death—how do the different characters deal with it? • How can love and frustration go hand in hand? • Comparison with Burningham's *Granpa*	• Use of photo-real illustration to position the reader and make direct eye contact • Use of facial expression to convey emotion often in contrast to what the written text is stating • Variety of facial expressions to indicate individual responses to death

Source: Anstey, M., & Bull, G. *Reading the Visual: Written and Illustrated Children's Literature* (pp. 243–245). Thomson Learning Australia, © 2000. Used with permission.

Each piece of advice is intended to create the possibility of different meanings that are realised through the multiple narratives contained in the book.

These three books are consciously postmodern, because the authors have chosen to construct the illustrative or written text in a particular way in order to encourage new readings (see Arizpe & Styles, 2003; Watson & Styles, 1996). The issue as to whether the picture book has been intentionally constructed along postmodern lines is not of central concern if the emphasis is on how the text might be read. The teacher should be concerned with how he or she might use the text or how the reader and viewer might approach it. The question of pedagogy with postmodern picture books comes in to play with regard to the new literacies. Because postmodern picture books require different ways of reading and viewing in order to uncover multiple meanings, they can provide experiences readers need that are central to the new literacies. Anstey (2002a) compared the understandings about text required to be multiliterate with the characteristics of postmodern picture books and found that the characteristics of postmodern picture books facilitate the development of multiliteracies. That comparison is detailed in Table 4. Table 4 shows that particular features of postmodern picture books can provide experiences and

TABLE 4
How Postmodern Picture Books Provide Experiences With the New Literacies

Required Understandings About Text to Be Multiliterate in the 21st Century	Corresponding Features of Postmodern Picture Books
All texts are consciously constructed and have particular social, cultural, political, and economic purposes.	• The postmodern picture book is consciously constructed to challenge and engage the reader in new and different ways. • Unusual uses of the narrator's voice position the reader and viewer to read the book in particular ways and through a particular character's eyes. (This can be achieved by the written or visual text.)
Text comes in a variety of representational forms incorporating a range of grammars and semiotic systems.	• A pastiche of illustrative styles requires the reader and viewer to employ a range of knowledge and grammar sets to read. • Changes to traditional book formats with new and unusual design and layout challenge reader and viewer perceptions of how to read a book.
Changes in society and technology will continue to challenge and change texts and their representational forms.	• The postmodern picture book is consciously constructed to challenge and engage the reader in new and different ways. • A pastiche of illustrative styles requires the reader and viewer to employ a range of knowledge and grammar sets to read. • Changes to traditional book formats with new and unusual design and layout challenge reader and viewer perceptions of how to read a book.
There may be more than one way of reading or viewing a text depending on a range of contextual and other factors.	• Unusual uses of the narrator's voice position the reader and viewer to read the book in particular ways and through a particular character's eyes. (This can be achieved by the written or visual text.) • Indeterminacy in written or illustrative text, plot, character, or setting requires the reader to construct some of the text and meanings. • Contesting discourses (between illustrative and written text) require the reader to consider alternate readings and meaning. • Intertextuality requires the reader and viewer to access and use background knowledge in order to access the available meanings. • Multiple readings and meanings provide for a variety of audiences.
There is a need to consider the possible meanings of a text, how they are constructing the person and the world around them in particular ways, and why this construction is being made.	• Unusual uses of the narrator's voice position the reader and viewer to read the book in particular ways and through a particular character's eyes. (This can be achieved by the written or visual text.) • Indeterminacy in written or illustrative text, plot, character, or setting requires the reader to construct some of the text and meanings. • Contesting discourses (between illustrative and written text) require the reader to consider alternate readings and meaning. • Multiple readings and meanings provide for a variety of audiences.

Source: Anstey, M. 'It's Not All Black and White: Postmodern Picture Books and New Literacies'. *Journal of Adolescent & Adult Literacy*, 45(6), p. 448. International Reading Association, © 2002. Adapted with permission.

understandings that support the development of a multiliterate individual who can participate as an active and fully functioning citizen of the 21st century. Such experiences and understandings can form the basis of a critical pedagogy that is dynamic and therefore more likely to adapt to cultural and technological change and evolving new literacies. In other words, the metafictive elements that distinguish postmodern picture books from other picture books are particularly helpful in supporting the development of the new literacies.

A feature of the new literacies is that they require a critical approach to literacy teaching and learning that views literacy as a dynamic, strategic, and problem-solving enterprise. Table 5 outlines some strategies that might be em-

TABLE 5
Postmodern Picture Books and Critical Pedagogy

Critical Pedagogy	Sample Implementation
Demonstrating to the reader that there is more than one literacy that needs to be learnt in order to read a text.	In the Australian picture book *Sand Swimmers*, written and illustrated by Narelle Oliver, there are three illustrative texts. This difference allows the reader to construct two different narratives in the text, one that relies on interpretation through visual literacy and one that relies more on the traditional print literacy. The three illustrative texts support the construction of further understandings about visual literacy and different semiotic systems.
Readers need to learn that texts can be problematic and can have multiple meanings. Meaning can therefore be up for negotiation rather than each text only having one correct meaning.	In the British picture book *Come Away From the Water, Shirley* by John Burningham, there is one meaning that can be constructed from the written text. However there are two illustrative texts on each spread, one that follows the activities of Shirley's parents and one that traces the adventures of Shirley and her imaginary pirate friends. These two illustrative texts create other alternative meanings. Finally, the interplay between the written text and the two illustrative texts creates a fourth meaning that explores the relationship between Shirley and her parents. All the meanings play a part in developing different meanings within the narrative and permit a number of interpretations of the text.
Students require experience with a range of different genres and semiotic systems and must be able to understand their codes and conventions.	In *Black and White* the U.S. author David Macaulay has interspersed the narrative genre with the comic form, recounts, and reports. The pastiche of illustrative styles creates four parallel narratives that have to be read and viewed simultaneously. The old rules of left to right and top to bottom in the semiotic system of print text no longer apply.
Texts do not always have a neat and tidy resolution but can have indeterminate endings that can lead to different meanings.	In the Australian picture book *The Rabbits* written by John Marsden and illustrated by Shaun Tan, the narrative ends with a question so that the reader is not presented with a straightforward resolution. This indeterminacy requires that the reader construct alternative endings to the narrative.
Texts often draw on other texts in order to construct meaning.	*The Rabbits* draws on meanings to be found in other texts (intertextuality). Readers will have more meanings available to them if they are aware of historical texts about early Australian history and if they have some experience with the genre of science fiction. With the illustrative text more meanings will be available if the viewer has some knowledge of different artistic styles, artists, and art history, and the part they played in the recording of Australian history.

Source: Bull, G. 'An Investigation of the Pedagogy of Literature: Using Literature to Support Learning'. In Anstey, M., & Bull, G. *The Literacy Lexicon* (2nd ed., p. 158). Pearson Education Australia, © 2004. Adapted with permission.

ployed to support the establishment of critical pedagogy. As shown in Table 5, critical pedagogy can be implemented through an appreciation that literacy (reading and viewing in particular in these examples) involves employing strategies from a problem-solving perspective. When picture books, and texts in general, require such different readings and produce a range of alternative meanings, the reader and viewer has to select the correct approach to the deconstruction and reconstruction of texts from a number of possible alternatives. This is a dynamic approach to learning and teaching through literacy that involves selecting certain strategies to deal with the solution of particular problems. Those problems fall into a whole range of new, multimodal texts that may contain still and moving images, sound, dialogue, and such elements as lighting and camera position. This approach is in apposition to more static approaches to literacy that rely on the application of a narrow range of tried and true activities across many literate practices in the belief that they will work in all situations. Such a one-size-fits-all view places too much reliance on a narrow range of overgeneralised techniques. Instead, literacy needs to be a dynamic, strategic, and problem-solving enterprise to cope with the vast array of new, multimodal texts that require familiarisation with a range of semiotic systems. Table 6 identifies some ways that particular picture books can be used to explore issues in critical reading. Picture books can be used to help students interrogate, or examine, the illustrative or written text from a critical perspective.

TABLE 6
Developing Critical Reading of Written and Illustrative Texts in Picture Books

Picture Book	Issues
Burningham, J. (1987). *John Patrick Norman McHennessy—The Boy Who Was Always Late*. Jonathan Cape, London.	Look at how the different constructions of learning and schools marginalises teachers.
Burningham, J. (1984). *Granpa*. Jonathan Cape, London. (Very useful to compare this to the 1990 *Granpa: The Book of the Film*. Red Fox, London, to see how the filmic genre has changed the narrative, the illustrative text, and some of the discourses.)	Two discourses (adult and child) signified by different fonts and illustrative texts. Also representation of past/present and imaginary/real in illustrative texts.
Baker, J. (1987). *Where the Forest Meets the Sea*. Julia MacRae, London.	A conservationist view of the world where humanity's impact on the environment (particularly 'progress') degrades the surroundings. How the environment has changed over recent times. *(continued)*

TABLE 6 (continued)
Developing Critical Reading of Written and Illustrative Texts in Picture Books

Picture Book	Issues
Baker, J. (1991). *Window*. Julia MacRae, London.	"
Baker, J. (1995). *The Story of Rosy Dock*. Random House, Sydney.	"
Wagner, J., & Brooks, R. (1977). *John Brown, Rose and the Midnight Cat*. Puffin, Melbourne. (Compare this book with other picture books written in the 1970s to see how different the illustrative and written texts are.)	Explores loneliness from the point of view of both John Brown and Rose. The character of Rose can be 'read' as either lonely or selfish.
Allen, P. (1986). *Herbert & Harry*. Nelson, Melbourne.	Presents a particular world view. Rich and poor characters are constructed in value laden ways and being rich or poor is presented as having certain effects upon characters.
Foreman, M. (1990). *War Boy*. Arcade, New York.	Constructs life in war torn Britain in the 1940s from a young child's (Foreman's) point of view. Presents a very Anglicised (almost authorised) world view from which alternate views could be derived.
Briggs, R. (1982). *When the Wind Blows*. Puffin, London.	One of the most powerful and terrifying anti-war books for children but is constructed around the milieu of the Cold War. Very reliant on a particular period in history but an in depth treatment of the relationship of an older married couple.
Marsden, J., & Tan, S. (1998). *The Rabbits*. Lothian, Melbourne.	Deals with an invasion of Australia but can be read in a number of ways—white invasion or alien or as an environmental/pollution problem—or all of these. Many possible readings.
Oliver, N. (1999). *Sand Swimmers: The Secret Life of Australia's Dead Heart*. Lothian, Melbourne.	A picture book with multiple written and illustrative texts all with their own purpose and none dominant. Contains many world views and different readings.
Say, A. (1993). *Grandfather's Journey*. Houghton Mifflin, Boston.	Bridges two cultures, American and Japanese, and therefore presents two world views with sometimes opposing attitudes and values.
Ferrier, S. (1984). *Ned: A Legend*. Collins, Sydney.	Authorises an alternate, and humorous, telling of the Ned Kelly story.
Waddell, M., & Eachus, J. (1994). *The Big Big Sea*. Walker Books, London.	Another book which can be read a number of different ways (including the silencing of men), e.g., As the child is now narrating the story as a memory is the father now missing or the mother?
Hest, A., & Lynch, P.L. (1997). *When Jessie Came Across the Sea*. Walker Books, London.	Re-creates life at the turn of the nineteenth century and also explores the relationships between grandparents and grand children. Examines the life of Jewish immigrants to America. Contains many different world views.

Source: Anstey, M., & Bull, G. *Reading the Visual: Written and Illustrated Children's Literature* (pp. 212–213). Harcourt Australia/Thomson Learning Australia, © 2000. Used with permission.

Summary: Reconsidering Picture Books in Terms of New Literacies

This chapter has examined the new literacies required to engage with new texts that are increasingly a part of our everyday lives. New conceptualisations of literacy, teaching, and learning are necessary to deal adequately with these new texts and develop a more critical pedagogy. The discussions in this chapter focussed on picture books, which require a reconsideration of the part that written and illustrative texts play in the creation of multiple meanings in narratives. Teachers also need to consider the part that different constructions of text play in creating alternative readings of stories. Although this chapter limited the discussions to narrative and the semiotic system of print, the next chapter explores still and moving images and the codes and conventions that make up their semiotic systems. This will reinforce the call for more critical pedagogies to cope with new literacies.

CHAPTER 5

The Consumption and Production of Text

This chapter investigates the characteristics of still and moving images within complex texts and explores how the codes and conventions of their semiotic systems can be manipulated to convey meaning. In this way teachers can develop better understanding of how texts are produced (written, scripted, or designed) or consumed (read, viewed, or realised) to accomplish their purpose and reconstruct reality. In other words, teachers can explore how text contributes to defining what they and their students see as reality.

How Texts Are Defined

Print Texts

Text can be defined as meaningful units of written, or print, language. This narrow and more conventional point of view (Lankshear, 1997) suggests that text is merely a passage of printed words. Such print texts can be termed *bounded* (Lankshear & Snyder, 2000), that is, what is bound up in those objects known as books. The linguistic semiotic system—the set of signs and symbols that form the basis of print text—was founded on what Lankshear and Snyder (2000) referred to as the 'lingering basics' (p. 63). Those basics included the fundamentals of decoding and encoding of sounds and essential understandings about the structures and syntax of sentences. These notions about text were adequate during what is now termed the industrial age. In the postindustrial age of the late 20th century, the increasing rate of technological innovation produced a plethora of new forms of text. With the advent of film, video, gaming, the Internet, and the increasing visual content in books and magazines came a whole range of texts that were not print based. In this new era of what has become known as the information age, or knowledge economy, this notion of text as only print might be seen as necessary but not sufficient. Knowledge of the linguistic semiotic system that is the basis of print text is still as necessary as it has always been, but in this highly visual and technological age it is no longer sufficient.

New Texts

With the appearance of new technology and new forms of media, print text is no longer the only basic. Although the great debate in literacy was once very much a question of which approach to reading (phonics or whole language) was most effective, with changing texts it becomes more a question of which text type (Arnold, 1996) might be the most effective or powerful. The diversity of text types has moved the debate away from one about method to one about exploration of semiotic systems. The following developments and trends (Anstey & Bull, 2004) indicate the variety of texts that now form part of everyday contemporary life:

- new modes of presentation, particularly those that rely on visual texts and visual literacy
- a range of media texts in film, video, and television
- multimodal texts that are the result of different combinations of modes such as visual, oral, and aural
- nonlinear arrangements of blocks of information that are linked to form hypertexts and hybrid texts
- different combinations of texts or texts that borrow from one another
- texts that originate from different social or cultural groups
- what Zammit and Downes (2002) refer to as 'unfiltered texts' (p. 25), which may be neither authentic nor credible

The greater variety of texts that are available has created greater speed and efficiency in the consumption and production of information, but it has also brought with it greater complexity. This complexity has foregrounded the issue of access to the new forms of text. Some social and cultural groups find themselves excluded through lack of personal or financial resources. Beyond questions of repertoire of personal experiences or adequate provision of technical equipment or the prerequisite hardware is the question of language. As Hawisher and Selfe (2000) suggest, some of the new text forms may require particular forms of culture-specific language or necessitate socially situated literacy practices that are not available to some social groups or cultures. There are particular lifeworlds (Cope & Kalantzis, 2000) that simply do not allow access to the new texts. Such a lack of resources creates issues that are far more basic than how texts might be interpreted, what the meanings in the text are, or how many meanings there are and to whom they are available.

Visual Texts

The information age is awash with text that is mediated through film, video, advertising, gaming, and the Internet. Contemporary students face a world far different from the print-saturated environment of their parents. In today's world, these new media texts are part of popular culture and are quite different from the more traditional texts associated with the canon of quality literature. As Watson and Styles (1996) suggested, students are now confronted with a variety of semiotic systems before they reach school. Young children may arrive at school being highly literate in unexpected ways. They may demonstrate sophisticated and well-developed levels of visual or technological literacy well before they become print literate.

This culture of the visual has focused attention on the connection between print text and visual text. Pullman (1989), Sipe (1998), Lewis (2001), Nikolajeva and Scott (2001), and Arizpe and Styles (2003) have all explored how meaning is created by the interrelationship of print and visual images and have highlighted the differences between the semiotic systems. The semiotic system associated with visual texts encompasses elements such as colour, line, format, texture, and shape that students need control over in order to make meaning. The added complication with visual text is that it can be produced as both still and moving images; therefore, students need to be aware of the codes and conventions that are employed in both forms.

Moving images also have a semiotic system and occupy a central part of literate practice. Film, videos, television, and cartoons are part of everyday life as never before, and this trend is augmented by new platforms such as the Internet and video games. These new sites also contain a high proportion of film, video, and cartoons and are often accompanied by music, voiceovers, and sound effects. This semiotic system relies on codes and conventions to interpret elements such as camera angle, lighting, gesture, setting, and dress. Often the reader and viewer has to contend with the codes and conventions of still and moving images to interact successfully with any given site. Full engagement is dependent on an individual's ability to operate across a number of different modes.

Multimodal Texts

Multimodal texts are those that rely on the processing and interpretation of print information, which blends with visual, audio, spoken, nonverbal, and other forms of expression produced through a range of different technologies. This blending produces hybrid texts that are frequently nonlinear (i.e., they no longer read from left to right or top to bottom) and often interactive and dynamic (e.g., through the inclusion of hyperlinks). The interactive nature of the text now allows the reader and viewer to select a highly individualised pathway to produce a hypertext, the text created by the reader by choosing his or her own pathway through a text such as a website in which multiple pathways are available. On other occasions the same reader may make different choices in negotiating the text and construct quite a different hypertext. The potential for creating different readings and viewings of the text is greatly increased. This refocuses attention on the relationship between the reader and the text and illustrates just how the reader is central to the creation of meaning in the text. New texts require new metalanguages to talk about them and require engagement in new forms of literacy. In the same way that identification and exploration of genres has developed as a way of talking about forms of writing, metalanguages are being developed to talk about texts. The codes and conventions of the semiotic systems of still and moving images are examples of the ways that teachers and students have to learn to talk about the new forms of text.

THEORY INTO PRACTICE: CLASSROOM APPLICATION

Following are two strategies to focus on ensuring (a) that you have a balance of texts in your classroom and (b) that the texts you use in the classroom reflect the lifeworlds of your students.

Activity 1

1. Complete a tally of the texts you use in your classroom over a week, their modes, and semiotic systems. The Use of Different Types of Text chart provides one suggestion for how you might do this with some initial entries:

Use of Different Types of Text

Subject	Print Text	Multimodal Text	Semiotic System
English	Class reader	Short film	Visual, auditory
	Chart	Video clip	Spatial, auditory, gestural
		Internet site	Visual, auditory, spatial, gestural
		Mobile phone	Auditory, visual, spatial
Mathematics	Set text Math exercise book		
Social science		Field trip	
Science		Experiment	
Health and physical education		Demonstration	
Art			
Technology			
The study of other languages			

It is important to look at all the subjects, not just English, and also to realise that nonprint texts can be live or electronic. Whatever the balance between print, live, and electronic texts you decide to strike in your classroom, the texts will need to reflect the lifeworlds of your students.

2. Check the balance between (a) print text and other forms of text, (b) oral and written forms, and (c) use of these texts in English lessons and other subject areas.

Activity 2

1. In order to compare how much your students learn through attending to still and moving images (e.g., film, video, comics, cartoons, magazines, the Internet, newspapers) in their home context and how often you use still and moving images for learning in your classroom, have each student fill in a diary of his or her day similar to the one represented in the Diary of Still and Moving Activities. Simplify it by requiring students to fill in the activities that they engage in at home before they come to school.

Diary of Still and Moving Activities

Daily Activity	Semiotic System Used	Reason for Use
Eating breakfast Reading cereal packets	Linguistic	Deciding which one to eat for breakfast based on number of calories
Reading newspaper	Linguistic, visual	Catching up with sports reports
Watching morning television news		
• Listening to news broadcast and reading accompanying print text	Auditory, linguistic	Finding out latest news
• Watching a video interview of politician	Visual	Checking where interview is taking place
• Attending to politician's message, looking at film clip, and watching body language	Auditory, visual, gestural	Trying to decide whether to believe message
• Looking at weather map, listening to forecast, attending to weather patterns on map, watching host	Linguistic, visual, auditory, spatial, gestural	Deciding whether to go for a picnic

2. You can then use these diaries at school to investigate how often the students engage in literate practices and what type of practices they

employ. You may find that your students use still and moving images in their literate practices more often than they use print texts. If so, you need to look at your pedagogy to see if you are teaching them about the codes and conventions of still and moving images as well as the codes and conventions of the linguistic semiotic system. This is not to suggest that the school curriculum has to be totally driven by what is happening in the students' lifeworlds, but it does mean that what is happening in your class has to have some relevance to the lives of your students.

The Interpretation of Texts

Making meaning from text emphasises the relationship between reader (or viewer) and text. Any interpretation of the text that the reader makes depends as much on what the reader brings *to* the text as what the reader takes *from* the text. The skills and processes that form part of the reading process impinge on what interpretations are made by the reader, but so do the different resources the reader brings to the text in the form of knowledge and experience. These resources form a repertoire that is drawn from an individual's lifeworld and school-based world (Cope & Kalantzis, 2000) and have a direct impact on any interpretation of text. As Barton (1994) suggests, interpreting text involves interaction with the text and not merely identifying the meaning of the text. He suggests that such interactions may be either life-to-text or text-to-life. In life-to-text interactions, the individual reader draws on life experiences. In the text-to-life interactions, the reader draws on knowledge about text as part of his or her literacy identity to enable successful engagement with text.

Interpretation requires a transformation of text read or viewed into another new text in the reader or viewer's head. This new text, authored by the reader or viewer, is a translation (Gee, 1992) of the original text and is necessary if meaning is to be successfully derived. This type of translation has a long history of research that has addressed the issue of how individuals effect changes in the text (Bakhtin, 1981; Barthes, 1975; Derrida, 1975; Said, 1983). For example, Arizpe and Styles (2003) found that students made transformations in visual texts by constructing what they termed *virtual texts*, which were the viewers' reconstructions of visual texts found in picture books using personal experience and imagination. New text is produced when the viewer converts the original text into a new text. In this case it is a visual text, but the same rules for the consumption and production of text apply as they did for print text.

Interpretation can be aided by the questions that educators ask of readers or by the readers taking on a critical perspective themselves. Either way, students can benefit from the stimulation of critical awareness with respect to texts. This can be achieved by asking the following types of questions (adapted from Bull, 2003) when producing or consuming text:

- Who produced this text?
- What is the purpose of this text?
- Who is this text produced for?
- Of what relevance is this text?
- Why is this topic being written about?
- From whose perspective is this text constructed?
- Are there other possible constructions from different points of view?
- Whose interests are being served by this text?
- Who is excluded or included in this text? Why?
- What assumptions about the potential audiences of this text have been made?
- Are there particular attitudes, values, and ideologies that are foregrounded in this text?
- Are there certain discourses that are valued?
- Who is silenced or marginalised by this text?
- Who is empowered by this text?
- Are any stereotypes represented or challenged?
- How might this text be transformed or reconstructed?

THEORY INTO PRACTICE: CLASSROOM APPLICATION

Use the list of questions above in different ways in the classroom.

1. Review your pedagogy. How well does the planning that you have done lend itself to exploration of the issues raised by the questions? Are you introducing strategies that will support learners dealing with issues such as who is marginalised or silenced by certain types of texts? If you were planning to make a study of advertising in newspapers or on television, have you organised to look at the way gender or race is represented (or not) in the advertisements or in the choice of people who are part of the scripts used?

2. Look at the range of texts that you use over a week and examine the constructions represented in these texts.

3. Look at individual lessons and make a study of the type of questions that you ask in and around texts and compare them against the list of questions provided in the previous section. Keep in mind that the terms *production* (instead of *writing*) and *consumption* (instead of *reading*) of text can be more easily applied to forms of text other than print. Although it is useful to talk about writing or reading a print text, it is more appropriate to talk about producing or consuming a visual text. Therefore, as you begin to use a greater variety of texts in your classroom you should introduce the terms that have a wider application and draw the attention of your students to the changes that you are making.

Having explored how texts are produced and consumed it is now possible to explore the particular cases of still and moving images.

Semiotic Systems

Past experience with print text has meant that most adult readers have a fairly detailed knowledge about the semiotic system of print text, which includes such elements as sight vocabulary, phrase, clause, parts of speech, traditional and functional grammar, and how sentences and paragraphs come together to form narrative, but little about the semiotic systems of illustration—specifically about still and moving images.

Semiotic systems are systems of signs that have shared meaning within a group, whether societal or cultural, that allow members to analyse and discuss how they make meaning. A semiotic system is, therefore, by definition, culture specific and may not be shared by every student in a classroom. Each system has its own codes and conventions—that is, individual elements that convey meaning and accepted ways in which the codes come together to make meaning. The use and application of the different codes and conventions of still images are particularly relevant in contemporary times because of the new texts in modern technological platforms.

The Semiotic System of Still Images

When William Caxton printed *Aesop's Fables* in 1484, it became a perennial favourite with children, although at the time it was meant to be a book for adults. At the outset, children were drawn to the act of reading much as they are today. What is surprising about this date is that parliamentary laws allowing all children the right to literacy education were only enacted in the late 19th century—some 400 years later. Before then, only the children of the rich and landed gentry were given access to literacy. Since then a considerable amount of time and energy has been spent teaching about reading the words—but rarely about reading the pictures. In fact, as students progressed through primary and secondary school, illustration in the fictional material available to them, both inside and outside of school, largely disappeared. Just a casual glance through a set of classroom reading texts illustrates the fact that as students progress through year levels, the number of illustrations decreases as the amount of print text increases. Only in factual or nonfiction texts do the illustrations remain in the form of diagrams, photographs, sketches, graphs, tables, and so on. It would be reasonable to expect that fiction material would contain proportions of illustrative texts similar to those in nonfiction material. It is also hard to justify why teachers spend so much time on the written text and so little time on the illustrative text. For whatever reason, getting meaning from the illustrative text is not emphasised anywhere nearly as much as with the print text.

A still image traditionally took the form of an illustration in a picture book, a picture in a magazine or newspaper, or a photograph. Still images can now be found on a website or mobile phone and can include any image that is not moving. A still image may contain some print or symbols as an adjunct, but it is predominantly pictorial. Students are constantly faced with still images in the variety of multimodal texts that make up a part of their normal day. Students need a vocabulary, or metalanguage, to talk about these images and how they assist in the construction of text, and how students can make meaning of them. The semiotic system of still images comes from the discipline of art and design (see Kress & van Leeuwen, 1990, 2001; Trifonas, 1998; van Leeuwen & Jewitt, 2001) and has its own codes and conventions. Figure 8 outlines a simplified version of the codes and conventions of the semiotic system of still images.

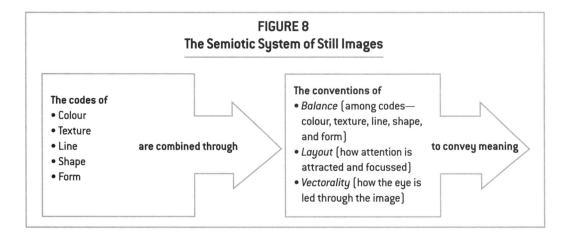

FIGURE 8
The Semiotic System of Still Images

The codes of
- Colour
- Texture
- Line
- Shape
- Form

are combined through

The conventions of
- *Balance* (among codes— colour, texture, line, shape, and form)
- *Layout* (how attention is attracted and focussed)
- *Vectorality* (how the eye is led through the image)

to convey meaning

To develop these ideas further, consider the example of line as a way to explore how meaning might be conveyed. Line can add emphasis in an obvious way by being thick or thin, heavy or light. However, it can also be used to convey mood or feelings. Table 7 explores the ways in which line can convey meaning. It is important to realise that these examples hold true only within western cultures and may represent entirely different meanings in other cultures.

Use of line in still images enables meanings to be communicated that would take a large amount of print text to convey. In picture books line can be used to create mood or feelings that are not portrayed, or only hinted at, in the

TABLE 7
Interpreting Line

Type	Example	Interpretation
Vertical		Isolation or a lack of movement Can suggest trees or people
Horizontal		Calmness, a lack of strife Can suggest a horizon or a water surface
Doorways		Solidity and security Can suggest doorways or buildings
Right angles		Manmade construction Can suggest artificial elements, unnatural phenomenon
Diagonals		Being off balance or out of control Can suggest falling objects
Jagged		Destruction or anger Can suggest lightning or eruptions
Curve		Less definite or predictable Can suggest water or fluid movement

Source: Anstey, M., & Bull, G. *Reading the Visual: Written and Illustrated Children's Literature* (p. 181). Harcourt Australia, © 2000. Adapted with permission.

written text. In the Australian picture book *The Very Best of Friends* (1989) by Margaret Wild, the illustrator, Julie Vivas, conveys the feelings of William the cat through the use of jagged and diagonal lines shown in Figure 9.

The written text reveals that William has been abandoned by his owner, but the full realisation of just how wild and disturbed he has become is to be found only in the illustrative text. The layout and balance of these lines add to this effect, and the way in which the lines converge into vectors, taking the eye through the illustration, reinforce the meaning contained in the illustration. Viewers of this book may miss the full meaning of the narrative if they do not have access to the codes and conventions of still images. The reader and viewer also needs to be consciously aware of how line is being used to develop different meanings. This is particularly so when readers are put in situations in which they are producers of text or need to move beyond mere passive consumption. They need to be able to articulate how meaning *is conveyed* by consuming (viewing) the illustrative text in the picture book and also how it *can be conveyed* by producing (drawing) still images that are to accompany the print text that they have constructed.

These same codes and conventions apply in many other contexts. During the war in Iraq in the beginning of the 21st century, the front page of a regional, state, and national newspaper in Australia published the same image, illustrating American soldiers giving aid to an injured Iraqi soldier. The codes and conventions served as a tool to help determine what it was about this image

FIGURE 9
Illustration From *The Very Best of Friends*

Source: Wild, M. *The Very Best of Friends* (J. Vivas, Ill.). Margaret Hamilton, © 1989. Used with permission.

(among the hundreds that were available) that caused it to be selected by editors across Australia in such disparate newspapers—which is a rare occurrence. The image drew its power from the use of vectors in the shape of a *V* to draw attention to the water being offered by one American soldier on the right, juxtaposed with a rifle-wielding American soldier on the left. The opposing lines of the vectors led the eye towards the captured Iraqi soldier on the ground. There were many features of this image that made it dramatic. But the vectors played an important part in shaping the reading and creating a mood and feeling of the brutality of war on the one hand and compassion on the other. Obviously elements such as colour, shape, or form were also present in the image and added to the overall effect, but the vector set seemed to be the dominant element.

THEORY INTO PRACTICE: CLASSROOM APPLICATION

This activity is designed to assist you in identifying how and when you use still and moving images in your classroom.

1. Using the information that you gathered from the Use of Different Types of Text chart (see page 103) and Diary of Still and Moving Activities (see page 104), make an estimate of the time you spend teaching about reading still images and the amount of time your students spend engaging with them in their lifeworlds.

2. How close should these two amounts of time be? Keep in mind that when you are estimating the amount of time you spend on still images you should not be concerned with how often you use them (e.g., in reading a story to the class) but how often you are teaching about the codes and conventions of still images.

There are many issues to consider when attempting the interpretation of still images in text. Table 8 lists some questions that might be asked when viewing still images. These questions employ four different perspectives to do with (1) knowledge of the codes and conventions, (2) constructing meaning through them, (3) knowing how and when to employ them, and (4) examining their use critically to determine what attitudes and belief systems they rely upon.

Table 8 focusses on the set of practices and resources from the Four Resource Model that Freebody and Luke (1990, 2003) attest students need to engage in successful literate practice. Attention to these questions illustrates how interpretation and analysis of still images can aid not only in the construction of meaning but also in the production and consumption of text.

TABLE 8
How to View Still Images

What do I need to know about the codes and conventions?	How do I use them to make meaning?
1. How do I crack this image using what I know about the codes of colour, texture, line, shape, and form? 2. How do the codes (colour, texture, line, shape, and form) relate singly and in combination, that is, through balance and layout? 3. How does this image relate to the other parts of this text that use other semiotic systems, for example, the written text, the overall layout of the text, the text as a whole, and other images?	1. How does my purpose for reading this image and the context in which I am reading it influence my meaning making? 2. How are the ideas in this image presented—through the objects in the image or the codes? 3. Are ideas presented through other parts of this text which use other semiotic systems; for example, the written text, the overall layout of the text, the text as a whole, and other images? 4. How are my meanings changed or influenced by the interaction of the still image with other parts of the text which use other semiotic systems, for example, the written text, the overall layout of the text, the text as a whole, and other images? 5. What prior knowledge and experiences might help me make meaning of this image; for example; knowledge and experiences with the topic or content, purpose and context, or about the use of colour, texture, line, shape, form, balance, and layout in shaping meaning? 6. Is this image interactive; am I expected to manipulate it in any way, and if so how does this affect my meaning making? 7. Are there other possible meanings and readings of this image?
How might I use this image in the production or consumption of text?	**How do I examine this image from a critical perspective?**
1. What is the purpose of this image and what is my reason for using it? Therefore, what aspects of the image should I be attending to? 2. How have the uses of this image shaped its composition, its content, the codes used to compose it, and its balance and layout? 3. How does the purpose of this image and my use of it influence the way in which I read and use it with other parts of the text; for example, the written text, the overall layout of the text, the text as a whole, and other images? 4. How should I use this image in this context? How might others use it? 5. What are my options or alternatives once I have viewed this image and the rest of the text?	1. Why was this image produced? 2. What do the codes and the ways in which they have been brought together to convey meaning tell me about the values, ideologies, and attitudes the creators or producers of this still image might be trying to convey? 3. What is this image suggesting that I believe or do? What beliefs and positions are dominant in the image, and what is silenced or absent? 4. Are the positions, attitudes, and beliefs presented in the image supported by other parts of the text; for example, the written text, the overall layout of the text, the text as a whole, and other images? If they are not, why might this be so, and how does this affect my meaning making? 5. What other positions or beliefs or attitudes might be offered? 6. Having viewed and analysed the still image, what action am I going to take?

Source: Anstey, M., & Bull, G. *The Literacy Labyrinth* (2nd ed., p. 294). Pearson Education Australia, © 2004. Used with permission.

THEORY INTO PRACTICE: CLASSROOM APPLICATION

This activity is designed to assist you in examining still images in picture books with your students.

1. Select a picture book that you have used with your class previously. By choosing a book that is known to your students you can draw their attention to the way that they used illustrations to make meaning without being conscious of how they did it.

2. Choose one of the codes of still images—such as colour, because it is easy to identify—for the analysis. Limit your discussion to just one of the sections in Table 8 when you first try this. The question 'What do I need to know about the codes and conventions?' is an ideal place to start because it looks specifically at breaking the codes.

3. In later lessons you can move on to the other three sections. Your long-term aim is that your students will attend to all four sets of questions simultaneously.

4. In follow-up lessons it is important to move away from picture books to magazines, newspapers, and photographs. It is also important to use nonfiction as well as fiction texts and to move into other subject areas such as science, geography, and history. Such exploration will focus students on how still images are used in both paper and electronic texts.

The Semiotic System of Moving Images

Moving images play a large part in students' lives through television, video, film, and gaming. Moving images have a semiotic system of codes and conventions that are in part dependent on those of still images. However, moving images have a set of codes and conventions that represent meaning in particular ways and have been thoroughly investigated by researchers such as Goodman and Graddol (1996), van Leeuwen (1996), Fiske (1987), and Mckee (2001). Although some writers tend to use different terms to describe the same effect, three terms are fairly common in describing the codes for the semiotic system of moving images: technical, screen, and auditory.

Technical codes are to do with the actual construction of the text, from shooting scenes to editing the film into its final form. Screen codes are to do with the actual images on the screen and how they are constructed for filming. They can be achieved in various ways, through conventional filming or in combination with editing and special effects. The purpose of auditory codes is to shape meaning making by drawing attention to, or adding further meaning to, the images on the screen. Sound or audio tracks can be in various forms, including music tracks, voice-overs, and special-effects sounds. These tracks can vary in volume and speed and can be soft or hard. Students of all ages are involved with determining meaning through interpreting still and moving images as part of their everyday lives. Teachers might be tempted at first thought to assume that still images are more the concern of young students and that moving images might be best left for older students. However, young students, even before they arrive at their first school, have experienced countless hours of film, video, and television and have been involved in the production and consumption of texts containing moving images. Therefore, all students can benefit from access to the codes and conventions of moving images (see Table 9 for a list of the three major codes with accompanying conventions).

TABLE 9
The Semiotic System of Moving Images

Codes	Conventions
Technical Codes • Point of view—high, low, and eye-level angle, soft and hard focus • Framing—long, medium, and close-up shots/views • Lighting—soft, hard, glaring, subdued, bright, dull, spot, backlight • Editing—parallel cutting, speed-up, slow motion, inserts • Pacing • Transition—fade to black, fade to white, dissolves, subtitles	Technical codes are used to further highlight and produce the screen codes and auditory codes.
Screen Codes • Setting and props • Costume • Physique and movement *Auditory Codes* • Sound • Dialogue • Nonverbal • Music • Silence	Screen codes and auditory codes are manipulated to represent the purpose and genre of the audiovisual text.

Source: Anstey, M., & Bull, G. *The Literacy Labyrinth* (2nd ed., p. 301). Pearson Education Australia, © 2004. Adapted with permission.

THEORY INTO PRACTICE: CLASSROOM APPLICATION

This activity is designed to assist you in examining moving images with your students in an introductory way.

1. To practice the use of the codes and conventions of moving images, select only a small number of scenes, making up about 30 seconds to a minute of real-time playing. This is all that is necessary to work with the codes, and any longer selection will make the activity too involved and too long. Use part of a film or video that you are currently incorporating into your teaching program or use a topical cartoon, advertisement, or episode from a weekly show on television.

2. Play the selection all the way through first with the sound turned off. This eliminates the auditory codes that the students will always focus on if given the chance. In this way you can focus on just one of the other codes, such as the point of view or position of the camera. By playing the selection all the way through it also means that when you play it a second time the students already know the content of the scenes you have selected and can therefore concentrate on the code you have focused on.

3. Introduce students to the codes by discussing how they affect meaning. For example, in a basketball game, top-down camera shots are used to show positional play and how it is constructed, whereas eye-level and bottom-up shots focus on the role of close-in play and individual players. In a primary school in Queensland, Australia, a year 4 class (8- and 9-year-olds) looked at the camera position in different sports in the 2004 Olympics and what effect this had on the viewers' understanding of how to play the sport being shown. As a side issue they also studied the gender effect in sports by looking at how camera position changed when women's beach volleyball was being shown as opposed to men's beach volleyball.

As with still images, moving images require access to the required vocabulary for talk to take place. These conversations rely on the development of a metalanguage—a language to talk about the language of moving or still images. This operates the same way as phrase, sentence, genre, and other elements of the metalanguage of written text. It is easier for students to make meaning with written language if they have learnt how to talk about it, and so it is for moving images. Through watching cartoons, television advertisements, and film, students learn the part that camera angle plays in the portrayal of character. For example, by engaging in talk about the point of view of the camera students can come to realise that characters viewed from bottom up by the camera appear larger and frightening or threatening. This effect can be supported by costume (black clothing), lighting, and focus (hard and sharp) and by the appropriate music (minor key) and sudden or loud sound effects. Approaching a discussion of point of view through the codes and conventions of moving images provides an excellent introduction to discussion of point of view in written narrative. A very useful analysis of how these elements can be explored using advertisements from television is provided by C. Luke (2003) when she investigates how the codes and conventions are applied differentially in gender contexts. Luke suggests that elements such as soft and hard focus, music, primary and soft colours, and close-ups and long shots are used in different ways in advertisements for products for males and females. What these examples illustrate is that the technical, auditory, and screen codes work separately and in concert to produce certain meanings.

Summary: Understanding How All Semiotic Systems Work

Knowledge of the ways in which the different semiotic systems work is as important when students are exploring still and moving images as genre is when they are investigating print through written language. In other words, line, colour, shape, form, and so on have their separate and combined effects for still images as do sentence structure, grammar, and vocabulary in written language. Because knowledge of semiotic systems is central to students' understanding of how meaning is constructed during the consumption and production of visual texts, teachers should consider the following aspects of a multiliteracies pedagogy:

1. The teaching of still and moving images is appropriate for students of all ages.

2. Terminology is something that teachers should not be afraid of using with students because, rather than confuse them, it actually helps both student and teacher to be more explicit about what they are viewing and producing.

3. The question of how different semiotic systems relate to meaning making is addressed by a strategic and problem-solving approach to reading and writing.

4. It is not a question of whether students are capable of engaging with meaning making in different semiotic systems but rather a question of finding the appropriate pedagogy. Students can learn the semiotic systems if teachers can find a way to teach them.

CHAPTER 6

Planning for Multiliteracies

The focus of this chapter is on planning for the teaching of multiliteracies in the elementary school. The main issues are of balance in planning and approach to planning. This chapter will not address questions of how to plan lesson by lesson because teachers already have detailed experience in this area. Teachers have local knowledge of what is most suitable for the community that they serve, and they also best know the needs of the students for whom they are responsible. The aim here is to develop a number of templates that teachers can use to determine whether they have achieved balance in planning. These templates are termed *auditing instruments* because they encourage a review of a sequence of lessons or units of work that have already been completed. The instruments also can be used in a wider context to investigate programs of work and approaches to planning. Consequently, the auditing instruments investigate three popular approaches to literacy teaching and learning: guided reading, outcomes-based planning, and the integrated curriculum. The final auditing instrument presented can be used to review a whole-school literacy plan.

Why Balance in Approach Is Important

Earlier chapters made the point that particular approaches to literacy teaching are necessary but not sufficient. Although an approach may serve a very useful purpose and be necessary for successful learning, it may not be sufficient. As a case in point, the learning of phonics is central to success in decoding. However, by itself, it is not sufficient as a program or approach to literacy teaching. No pedagogy is sufficient by itself even though it may be essential in certain contexts or for particular purposes. The same holds true for planning. Specific approaches to planning suit certain purposes but are not sufficient for all occasions. Although it would be convenient for teachers if one planning approach would suffice, this would negate existing knowledge about individual differences in students and the effect of purpose and context. To assume that one approach will always work is to presume that one size fits all. Teachers need to look critically at the planning that they engage in, and the approaches that they use, to ensure a balance across possible methods.

Development of Auditing Instruments

Choosing appropriate auditing instruments depends on the particular balance a teacher is trying to achieve and also on the material he or she is trying to balance. This chapter presents six instruments that teachers may wish to implement in their classrooms for different purposes. They are by no means the only ones that teachers could employ and serve only as examples for teachers to generate their own.

Auditing Instrument for the Four Resource Model

Teachers can use the auditing instrument for the Four Resource Model to re-examine the ways they have been teaching literacy. It can be very useful if teachers want to follow the necessary but not sufficient idea of reviewing their planning to see if they are relying on only one method of literacy instruction. In some cases the same objective is repeated, for example, if a teacher is practicing a new skill or strategy or dealing with a group of students who need repeated instruction in a particular area. More often, however, teachers will want to determine whether they have balanced the use of certain methods over time. Table 10 represents a simple instrument that can be used to audit your planning to judge whether you have been overly relying on one aspect of the Four Resource Model, thus limiting the range of strategies for reading your students acquire.

TABLE 10 Four Resource Model Auditing Instrument	
Activities and materials in which the student is engaged primarily as a **meaning maker**, drawing on prior knowledge to make literal and inferential meaning.	Activities and materials in which the student is engaged primarily as a **code breaker**, breaking the code of a variety of semiotic systems to make sense of the marks on the page.
Activities and materials in which the student is engaged primarily as a **text user**, using the text as part of a real-life reading situation.	Activities and materials in which the student is engaged primarily as a **text analyst**, gaining understanding about how texts work, why they have been constructed, and how they shape values and attitudes.

THEORY INTO PRACTICE: CLASSROOM APPLICATION

Activity 1
Use Table 10 to review the use of the Four Resource Model in your classroom.

1. Examine a recent unit of work and code each activity as being mainly about one of the Four Resource Model practices: code breaker, meaning maker, text user, or text analyst.

2. Use the following questions to audit the balance among the four areas:

   ▸▸ Have I been engaging my students only in decoding or literal and inferential comprehension?

   ▸▸ Have I been asking my students to use the strategies I have taught them?

   ▸▸ Am I asking my class to make critical judgments about what they read?

   ▸▸ Have my students practiced strategies from the Four Resource Model with texts of a variety of modes and semiotic systems?

Activity 2

Use Table 11 to review the range of reading materials that you use with your classes. This will assist you to establish whether you have a balance in the approaches you use in reading instruction with the materials in your classroom. It is tempting to continue to use the same materials in the same way if you have found them successful in the past and you have completed all your preparation around them. The following steps can help you decide if you have a balance of materials.

1. Familiarise yourself with the reading materials, including teachers' manuals, textbooks, activity books, and blackline masters. Identify one set of materials or a textbook that you wish to analyse.

2. Using the Auditing Instrument of the Four Resource Model's reading practices in Table 11, make notes about or simply tick the dominant reading practices or resources that would be utilised while engaging with these materials or activities.

3. Briefly examine the philosophy about reading identified in your teachers' manual. If the philosophy is not stated overtly, you may be able to infer it from instructions to the teacher and other statements in the manual. Note which of the four reading practices are foregrounded.

4. Look at the balance on your grid. Which of the four resources is dominant? What does that mean in terms of using these materials in your classroom? How might you modify, add to, or change the use of these materials to correct the imbalance?

5. Consider the different approaches to the teaching of reading that you are aware of. Do the materials you have just analysed reflect any approach in particular? What are the implications of this for your use of these materials?

6. Do you need to seek out other materials or update your knowledge about different approaches to reading instruction?

Following the ideas outlined in Activity 1 (see pages 118–119), Jill Temple, a teacher at Middle Ridge, a school in Queensland, Australia, with her colleague Ray Lecky revised a series of lessons she had originally devised using Mother's Day catalogues to investigate how mothers were portrayed in terms of social class, ethnicity, age, and appearance. The objective was to change the pedagogy so that it catered for the teaching of the Four Resource Model and multiliteracies. The revised approach is illustrated in Table 11. You may find

---

TABLE 11
Using the Auditing Instrument for the Four Resource Model

The Four Resource Model

Code Breaker	Meaning Maker
Resources that enable the reader to crack the code of the written and visual text and determine how it works and what its patterns and conventions are: essentially, how do I crack this code? • How do I crack this text? • How does it work? • Is there more than one semiotic system operating here? If so, how do they relate? • What are the codes and conventions used? • How do the parts relate singly and in combination?	Resources that enable the reader to access the literal or implied meaning of the text and utilize his or her socio-cultural background to make meaning: essentially, what does this mean to me? • How are the ideas in this text sequenced—do they connect with one another? • Is the text linear or nonlinear, interactive or noninteractive? • How does this affect the way I make meaning? • How will my purpose for reading and the context in which I am reading influence my meaning making? • Are there other possible meanings and readings of this text?
Text User	Text Analyst
Resources that enable the reader to determine and fulfil his or her role in using the text: essentially, what do I do with this text? • What is the purpose of this text, and what is my purpose in using it? • How have the uses of this text shaped its composition? • What should I do with this text in this context? • What will others do with this text? • What are my options or alternatives after reading?	Resources that enable the reader to critically analyse the construction of the text in terms of the author's intentions, ideologies, inclusions, and omissions. Includes transformation: essentially, what does this text try to do to me? • What kind of person with what interests and values produced this text? • What are its origins? • What is the author/producer of this text trying to make me believe or do? • What beliefs and positions are dominant or silenced in the text? • What do I think about the way this text presents these ideas and what alternatives are there? • Having critically examined this text, what action am I going to take? • The 'so what' factor.

(continued)

TABLE 11 (continued)
Using the Auditing Instrument for the Four Resource Model

The Four Resource Model

Code Breaker
Identify the words and captions used in the advertising material. Compile a list, identifying captions used in each catalogue, radio ad, or TV ad.

Big W	My mother is special Just for mother Famous brand gifts to make Mother's Day
Target	For every style of mother All things for mother Give mother something special

Meaning Maker
View the different forms of advertising again. Discuss this topic or Think/Pair/Share the following statement:

'I'd buy my mother a gift from ___ because ___'

Think about what the still (brochures) and moving (TV ads) images mean to you.

Look through the catalogues; make a list of gift ideas for mother.

What is the purpose of Mother's Day advertising?

Compare the catalogues and discuss similarities and differences. Also do this with different radio or TV ads.

Text User
Get students to survey their mothers.
1. Make a list of what things your mother would really like for Mother's Day.
2. Ask your mother how she likes to be made to feel special. List her responses.

Discuss and collate the class responses. Encourage students to make statements based on their observations of advertising for Mother's Day. Create your own Mother's Day message in a presentation format of your choice (PowerPoint, poem, picture, painting, song, etc.).

Design a brochure advertising things your mother would like. Think of a catchy slogan you could use.

Text Analyst
Get students to critically analyse the Mother's Day advertising.
1. What types of products are they trying to sell? Does this match the class list of what mothers really want?
2. Which advertisement best matches your mother? Does it advertise in a way that would appeal to your mother? (Consider whether the ad was presented as a still or moving image. Discuss effectiveness of the medium used.)
3. Consider this statement—'Mother's Day is a gimmick. It was created by shops to try to sell more goods'.

Consider the different representations of women and stereotypes (e.g., book titles, DVD, beauty products).

Do you think they portray all women's groups?

Do the models represent women of all ages and body build?

In the U.K. they call it 'Mothering Day'. Why do you think they have done this? Discuss.

Why do catalogues such as Repco not use Mothers' Day to help them sell their products?

Source: Jill Temple and Ray Lecky. Used with permission.

this example useful when you use Table 10 to revise some of your planning. Details to notice specifically are the incorporation of the four practices and also the use of texts other than print. By including live and electronic texts it becomes possible to look at the codes and conventions of still and moving images.

Auditing Instrument for Texts

The history of the teaching of literacy has largely been about the teaching of print text. As discussed in chapter 4, the role of illustration in meaning making with print text has been minor from learning and teaching points of view. Therefore, teachers need to move into other semiotic systems as well as broaden their ideas about what form text itself can take. Text in its print form has played a central role in the lives of students and in classrooms (i.e., in lifeworlds and school-based worlds) for some hundreds of years. However, as discussed in chapter 1, various factors such as social, technological, and cultural change have combined to foreground the place of electronic and live text. With print, electronic, and live texts different semiotic systems come into play. The instruments included in this chapter can audit semiotic systems and text types, and they can be used in conjunction with one another. In each case teachers can use the instrument to determine the balance in planning with regard to text types and semiotic systems. It is no longer appropriate to rely only on print text and the linguistic semiotic system because individual lives, workplaces, occupations, and recreational pastimes have moved beyond what were once regarded as the basics to the new basics.

Table 12 shows an instrument for establishing a balance in the range of texts teachers use in planning or in the classroom. When teachers audit their planning they should not just conduct a simple count of how often they use items such as newspapers or film. It is appropriate for teachers to count when they are actually teaching the specific features of a particular text, what semiotic systems are involved with the use of such a text, and what codes and conventions come into play.

TABLE 12
Auditing Instrument for Texts

Text Type	Where and How Often Used
Print text (e.g., newspaper, book)	
Live text (e.g., person to person, live performance, artwork)	
Electronic text (e.g., mobile phone, computer)	

Auditing Instrument for Semiotic Systems

The auditing instrument in Table 13 was developed to check on balanced use of the various semiotic systems over time. In day-to-day practice teachers need to move away from a focus only on the linguistic semiotic system and print text with its emphasis on such things as grammar and genre. In a multiliterate classroom the other semiotic systems must form an important part of planning for the teaching and learning of literacy.

This goal does not mean that every lesson should contain all text types and involve discussion about all semiotic systems. Both the auditing instruments for texts and for semiotic systems should be used to look at patterns in planning over time. It would be appropriate for teachers to use these instruments to study their planning over a week at a time. If a week has passed and the teacher has looked only at print or at the linguistic semiotic system, then this is cause for concern. As a basis for comparison the teacher can make a judgment about the variety in these two areas in the lifeworlds of the students.

TABLE 13
Auditing Instrument for Semiotic Systems

Semiotic System	Where and How Often Used
Linguistic (oral and written language that uses vocabulary, generic structure, grammar, etc.)	
Visual (still and moving images that use colour, vectors, viewpoint, etc.)	
Auditory (music and sound effects that use volume, pitch, rhythm, etc.)	
Gestural (facial expression and body language that use movement, speed, stillness, etc.)	
Spatial (layout and organisation of objects in space that use proximity, direction, position, etc.)	

THEORY INTO PRACTICE: CLASSROOM APPLICATION

In Australia, the United Kingdom, and the United States in recent years, guided reading has become very popular. As with all new trends in literacy teaching and learning, guided reading has been implemented in different ways in different schools and systems. Not all versions of guided reading are the same, and not all schools follow the guidelines suggested by proponents. It is very informative to use the auditing instruments for texts and semiotic systems to look at the balance of strategies commonly used in this approach. The activities here include some strategies suggested in three works often cited by proponents of guided reading: Hornsby (2000) from Australia, Bradbury and colleagues (1997) from Australia, and Fountas and Pinnell (2001) from the United States.

Activity 1

If the following strategies were used in a classroom over a period of time, would they provide a balanced program? That is, would they achieve a balance of text types and semiotic systems? Use the two auditing instruments from Tables 12 and 13 to check. Outline the way you would teach lessons and which materials you would use and then apply the auditing instruments to the lesson outlines.

- Recognise and name the letters of the alphabet.
- Read orally and silently.
- Use letter–sound relationships and language structures to gain meaning.
- Use an index, glossary, and table of contents.
- Read signs in classroom and school contexts.
- Use title and illustrations to predict what will happen in the narrative.
- Reread text orally or silently.
- Ask questions about content of narrative or characters' feelings.
- Make a study of vocabulary, linguistic features, layout, and so forth.

After applying the auditing instruments, you will find that there is little mention of semiotic systems other than the linguistic and a narrow range of texts used. All of the strategies are for reading and do not consistently employ the other modes of listening, writing, and speaking. This does not mean that the strategies are poorly designed. In fact, they are very good at achieving the objectives that they were designed for as part of a reading program. What it does mean is that you as the teacher need to be aware of what these strategies are useful for. The problem is not with the strategies or with guided reading, but with the way they are implemented by the teacher or the school. If these strategies are the only ones you use in your guided reading program or anywhere else, then you do not have a balance in your planning.

Now, look at your planning for literacy teaching (not just the teaching of reading). Apply the two auditing instruments from Tables 12 and 13 on pages 122 and 123 to an overview of your planning and the strategies you are using. Look to see what variety of texts you have included and the semiotic systems that you have incorporated into your program. Now make a judgment about the balance in your planning.

Auditing Instrument for Learning Focus

The Use of Backward Mapping in Outcomes-Based Approaches to Planning

There are many possible starting points in deciding how to structure a sequence of lessons or a whole unit of work when there is a focus on student learning. Conventionally, it is possible to begin the process of planning by specifying what strategies the students are to learn and then consulting with the recommended syllabus or curriculum documents to see where these strategies might fit. The strategies then provide the focus around which the learning and teaching take place. Alternatively, it is also possible to begin with the general aims or goals of the relevant documents and work backwards. This type of process is often referred to as backward mapping. It involves the school or individual teacher beginning with the end point (the goals of the syllabus documents) and working back to individual lessons that will encourage the necessary learning and teaching. Figure 10 illustrates the processes

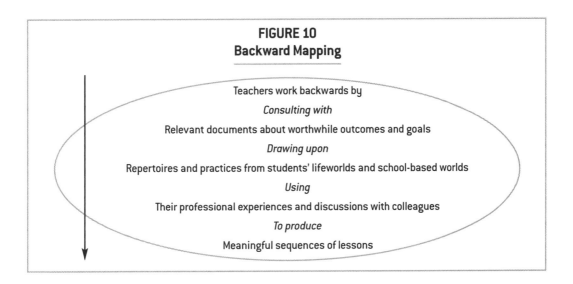

FIGURE 10
Backward Mapping

Teachers work backwards by

Consulting with

Relevant documents about worthwhile outcomes and goals

Drawing upon

Repertoires and practices from students' lifeworlds and school-based worlds

Using

Their professional experiences and discussions with colleagues

To produce

Meaningful sequences of lessons

that teachers might engage in to complete this type of planning. The words in italics represent the processes in planning that teachers engage in while they interact with each set of documents or data.

In recent times there have been a number of process curricula that have defined the processes that students are to learn rather than the more traditional content curricula that specified particular facts or knowledge. By working backwards from these processes it is possible to design lesson sequences that will produce the required type of learning. Determining balance in a process-based curriculum can be achieved by designing an auditing instrument that details those processes that have been judged to be central to the documents that have been authorised or legislated. A possible list of processes that could be incorporated into such an instrument appears in Table 14.

Determining balance in a content-based curriculum can be problematic because it is not feasible to design a manageable auditing instrument by specifying the required content. Part of the reason why outcomes-based curricula have become popular is that they try to bridge the gap between the content- and process-based curricula by defining a number of outcomes that specify both process and content. Table 15 is an example of planning using an outcomes-based approach. This planning was undertaken by a group of teachers (Moira Blackburne, Janelle Prouatt, Christine Berry, Gerald Livsey, Judy Chapman, and Dianne McDonough) at Raceview, a school in Queensland, Australia.

TABLE 14
Auditing a Process-Based Curriculum

Processes	Where and How Often Used
Researching	
Analysing	
Synthesising	
Negotiating	
Generalising	
Designing	
Judging	
Evaluating	
Communicating	

TABLE 15
Outcomes-Based Planning

Core Outcomes	Drama 2.1: Students make choices and develop roles to build dramatic action. Music 2.1: Students aurally and visually recognise and respond to Level 2 core content in music they hear and perform. Visual Arts 2.1: Students make images and objects by selecting and manipulating elements and additional concepts.
Processes	Making, performing, and responding
Pedagogical Overview	Supportive Classroom Environment • Student direction Do students determine specific activities or outcomes of the lesson? (deliberation/negotiation between teacher and students over the task of producing a backdrop for the play) • Explicit quality performance criteria Are the criteria for judging the range of student performance made explicit? (teachers make clear to students criteria for assessing levels of participation and communication during rehearsal and performance of the play) • Academic engagement Are students engaged and on-task during the lesson? (as above)
Multiliteracies	The students will • Read and enjoy Australian Illustrated Literature through the many stories of Mem Fox. • Publish story endings on the computer. • Use clip art to produce a greeting card, poster, advertisement, invitation. • Experience a range of literacy acts while preparing for and enacting a play.
Content Focus	The Magic of Stories • Investigating stories and books. • Exposure to authors including Mem Fox, Anna Feinberg, Robin Klein, Emily Rodda, and other Australian authors. • Introduce the narrative genre, including basic story and play. • Develop understanding of structure of genre, including decontextualising of narrative texts. • Innovate on texts to create new endings on existing stories. • Create and compose own story endings in published form. • Create a cooperative and supportive environment in which the class play is practiced. • Participate in music and drama activities with music specialist teacher to create a finished product.

(continued)

127

English Focus

Reading

Choose texts that are context specific.

- Guided reading sessions for Code Breaker (CB), Text Analyst (TA), Text Participant (TP), and Text User (TU)
- Cloze activities
- Read and retell (TP)
- Shared reading (CB, TU)
- Draw it out, act it out (TP)
- Story map (TP)
- Directed reading/thinking activities (TU)
- Reflection (TU)
- Oral reading of play (TU)
- Group reading of playlets (TU)

Writing

- Modelling and joint construction of narrative genre. (TP)
- Discussion and joint construction of new endings for existing stories. Innovations on texts. (TA)
- Draft, edit, and proofread own innovation. (CB)
- Publish final draft on the computer. (TU)

Source: Unit on the magic of stories by Moira Blackbourne, Kathy Dawes, Gerald Livsey, and Stacey Wratten. Used with permission.

A number of strengths in this type of planning can be determined by attending to the table itself. A selection of outcomes has been specified in order to strike a balance between process and content. These outcomes are supported by an overview of pedagogy that gives direction to teachers. The content and processes to be covered have also been clearly stated. Further to this has been specification of what area of multiliteracies is being covered and how the Four Resource Model is integrated into the planning process. The end result is a unit that is balanced in terms of a number of the auditing instruments discussed.

Not obvious in Table 15 is how the stated outcomes were selected. The outcomes-based approach that the teachers were attempting to deal with had prescribed a large number of outcomes. The teachers were concerned that if they tried to implement all of the outcomes spelt out in the documents that it would be 'death by a thousand outcomes'. The school made the decision to select only those outcomes that were pertinent to their situation and then to group the remaining ones in meaningful sets. This still allowed for the specificity that is one of the strengths of an outcomes-based approach and encouraged the teachers to be involved in goal setting as part of their planning. It did not, however, permit outcomes to totally drive the whole educational enterprise in the school. There was still balance in the planning process that provided space for such important features as pedagogy, multiliteracies, and the Four Resource Model. This balance can be addressed through the use of the auditing instruments.

THEORY INTO PRACTICE: CLASSROOM APPLICATION

Activity 1

If you are engaged in an outcomes-based approach you may wish to follow the same selection process as the teachers at Raceview.

1. Select only those outcomes that are applicable to your school context. Such a selection would have to involve the whole school and also perhaps the network of schools or district that your school is part of. (Many schools and districts have made the decision that the stated outcomes are a guide from which appropriate items can be selected. This may, or may not, be possible in your situation depending on how much autonomy there is at your district level.)

2. Group the remaining outcomes into meaningful sets in the same way that the Raceview teachers did.

3. Use these groups of outcomes as part of the planning process. You may wish to use the Raceview example as a model.

Activity 2

Once you have completed planning a unit of work, employ some of the auditing instruments described in Tables 10–13 to see if there is a balance in your planning. Remember that your planning does not need to be balanced in terms of all of these auditing instruments all of the time. However there does need to be coverage of the instruments over time. If, for example, in your last two units of work there was no mention of multiliteracies or of semiotic systems other than the linguistic, then there is probably a lack of balance in your planning.

The Use of Backward Mapping in the Integrated Curriculum

The idea of an integrated curriculum underwent a resurgence in the 1970s with the advent of the Literacy Across the Curriculum movement. This movement acknowledged that literacy was a part of all curriculum areas and that the teaching of literacy in curricula other than English enabled literacy to be taught in meaningful contexts. This led to the popularity of themes that linked all of the Key Learning Areas (KLAs), a term used in Australia to describe the essential curriculum areas, through the use of a focus on a particular topic or children's book. More recently in Australia, the integrated curriculum has resurfaced in many forms. Two of the most common forms have been the Rich Task and New Basics approaches. In the Rich Task approach there has been an attempt to define a series of tasks that enable integration of the curriculum to occur and, at the same time, still be relevant to students' lifeworlds and address the concerns of the prevailing literacy curriculum documents. The important features of the rich tasks are that they are authentic and relevant to the students' lives and that they are cognisant of the curriculum. This was not always the case with planning centred on themes in which the desire to link certain KLAs sometimes became more important than content or curriculum. An example of how the Rich Task approach to planning might be applied is shown in Figure 11. You can see that this particular approach also draws on outcomes-based approaches in the planning cycle that has been developed.

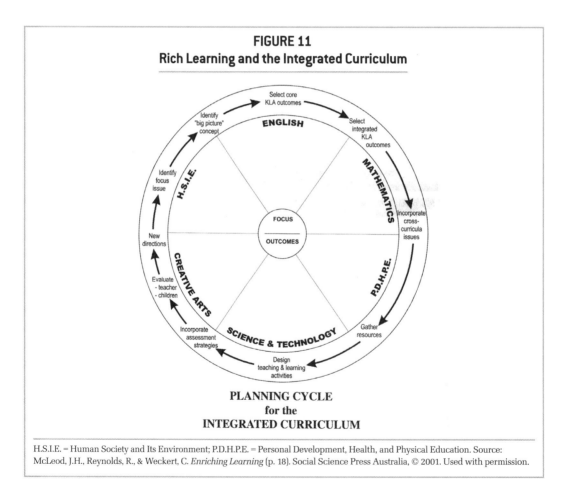

FIGURE 11
Rich Learning and the Integrated Curriculum

PLANNING CYCLE
for the
INTEGRATED CURRICULUM

H.S.I.E. = Human Society and Its Environment; P.D.H.P.E. = Personal Development, Health, and Physical Education. Source: McLeod, J.H., Reynolds, R., & Weckert, C. *Enriching Learning* (p. 18). Social Science Press Australia, © 2001. Used with permission.

In the New Basics approach to integration of the curriculum the focus is on redefining the KLAs so that the emphasis is on a series of rich projects or rich tasks that the students complete over the period of their time in elementary school. The tasks are designed to be transdisciplinary, concentrating on different types of learning, and often involve a narrowing of the number of KLAs, hence the name New Basics. Such an approach is illustrated in Figure 12. This curriculum model brings together different types of learning and a reconsideration of the notion of KLAs while at the same time still allowing for the inclusion of multiliteracies and a range of semiotic systems.

If you apply the auditing instruments from Tables 10–13 to the models in Figure 12 you can see where the balance is achieved. If you are using some form of the Integrated Curriculum in your school or classroom, then it might be quite useful to compare it with the Rich Task and New Basics approaches just reviewed. These two models are excellent examples of planning. They may not satisfy all the requirements of each of the four auditing instruments, but this does not mean that they are somehow defective in the approach to planning they are advocating. Both the Rich Tasks and New Basics approaches have their own strengths. As previously noted, it is a question of purpose and context. You apply the auditing instrument that is appropriate for the goals you have in mind.

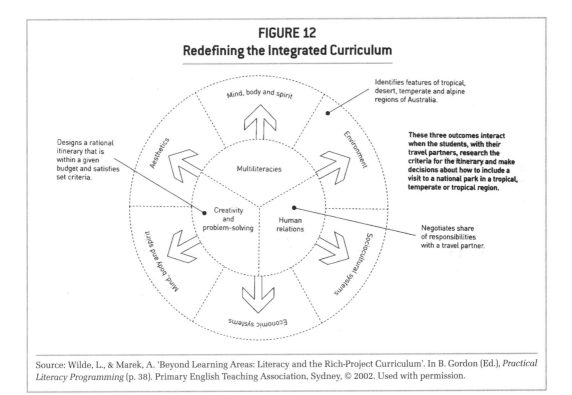

FIGURE 12
Redefining the Integrated Curriculum

Source: Wilde, L., & Marek, A. 'Beyond Learning Areas: Literacy and the Rich-Project Curriculum'. In B. Gordon (Ed.), *Practical Literacy Programming* (p. 38). Primary English Teaching Association, Sydney, © 2002. Used with permission.

You may also find it useful to apply the auditing instruments from Tables 10–13 to the version of the integrated curriculum that you are implementing to judge for yourself if you have a balanced approach, or alternatively, where the imbalances occur.

Auditing Instrument for Evaluating Pedagogy

The discussion has touched on the use of backward mapping at the general level and applied it to units of work or sequences of lessons. Backward mapping can also be used at the specific lesson level (as discussed in chapter 3). The auditing instrument shown in Table 16 can be used at the level of evaluating a teacher's pedagogical approach. It can be used to check if there is a balance in the content selected and also to examine the range of different pedagogies that the teacher has incorporated into his or her program.

For example, to use this instrument teachers might check in the knowledge area to see if they are teaching only facts or also definitions or understandings. In terms of the balance of pedagogy it is useful for teachers to check if they are always using direct instruction or employing other approaches such as learning through discovery.

TABLE 16
Auditing Instrument for Evaluating Pedagogy

Content of Task or Program	Where and How Often Applied	Pedagogy Used
Knowledge • Understandings • Facts/definitions • Terminology/vocabulary		
Processes • Strategies • Thinking skills • Decision making		
Behaviours • Collaboration • Question and answer • Negotiation		
Technological knowledge • Platform (e.g., mobile phone) • Software		

Activity 1
Use the auditing instrument in Table 16 to check the balance of the different pedagogies you are using. Remember that these pedagogies should vary within a particular area such as knowledge but also between areas. It is just as important to investigate how you change your pedagogical approach when teaching in the other areas of processes, behaviours, and technological knowledge.

Activity 2
An alternative use of this instrument is to vary the heading in column three. Instead of Pedagogy Used you may wish to substitute other headings such as Teacher Talk Employed, Phases of Lessons Used, or Materials Used.

Auditing Instrument for a Whole-School Literacy Plan

This auditing instrument focuses on the whole school because the strength of what happens in individual classrooms both affects, and is affected by, what is happening at the school level. Successful schools have shared two characteristics that appear to be essential in developing the school as a whole community. They have articulation from one year level to another, so as students progress through the school there is continuity. This continuity depends on the willingness of teachers to talk to one another and share their successful (and not so successful) practices. Space and time need to be created by administrators in order to encourage teachers to share their journeys. They also have a shared vision about the goals of the school and the pedagogies that are employed by the teachers. Again, without this shared vision, there can be little continuity. This does not mean that all teachers have to teach the same things in exactly the same way. What it does mean is that there have to be conversations going on throughout the school among all the teachers, so there is some commonality in beliefs about what the school is doing in general and about literacy teaching and learning in particular.

In order to begin the process of developing a shared vision and encouraging conversations among teachers, consult the auditing instrument with a whole-school perspective in Table 17. The instrument focuses on the resources, both intellectual and social, that students, teachers, and schools might draw on when questions about curriculum, pedagogy, and assessment arise. There is a dual emphasis on planning and whole-school approaches in order to explore the question of overall balance in school programming. There are a series of questions to be answered in each section of the

TABLE 17
Auditing Instrument for a Whole-School Literacy Plan

Social and Intellectual Resources Accessed	Curriculum	Pedagogy Used	Student Assessment and Teacher Validation
Students	When producing and consuming texts, do students draw on their lifeworld experiences? Do students see texts as part of their social and cultural practices?	Are students gaining access to a range of texts and semiotic systems? Do students use the codes and conventions and the metalanguages of the various semiotic systems?	Do the assessment tasks address real audiences and incorporate authentic tasks? Are assessment tasks related to both the school-based worlds and lifeworlds (literacy identities) of students?
Teachers	Does teacher planning draw on the lifeworlds of students as well as their school-based worlds? Does teacher planning include experience with semiotic systems; print, live, and electronic texts; and a range of multimodal texts?	Are all teachers familiar with a range of texts and semiotic systems? Are all teachers familiar with the codes and conventions and the metalanguages of the various semiotic systems?	Do the teacher-constructed assessment tools incorporate a range of auditing instruments that are designed to measure student progress in the new literacies and with the new texts? Are teachers developing instruments that will measure and validate change in teacher practice? Is there a balance between student assessment and teacher validation?
Schools	Does whole-school literacy planning address the consumption and production of a wide range of oral, print, multimodal, and electronic texts? Does whole-school literacy planning take account of the lifeworlds, as well as the school-based worlds, of students?	Does whole-school literacy planning identify the various texts, semiotic systems, and metalanguages and suggest strategies for teaching and learning them throughout the whole school?	Does whole-school literacy planning incorporate regular monitoring of the curriculum and pedagogies in use throughout the school? Does whole-school literacy planning incorporate validation of teacher practice in order to provide an overview of schoolwide pedagogy?

Source: Earlier version of the instrument developed by Sybil Bell for Education Queensland. Adapted with permission.

instrument to give some indication of balance. These are by no means the only questions that can be asked about Literacy Plans, but they are intended to provide a beginning perspective from which teachers can develop other vantage points to explore balance throughout the school.

THEORY INTO PRACTICE: CLASSROOM APPLICATION

Activity 1
Use the auditing instrument in Table 17 to check the balance in your literacy plan at the whole-school level. You may not wish to use all the questions in each section, but you should cover all the sections. It is important not to favour teachers over students and to cover issues related to curriculum, pedagogy, and assessment.

Activity 2
An alternative use of this instrument is to vary some of the questions so that you may address the particular concerns that your school is attempting to explore.

Summary: Balancing Our Pedagogy

Some of the central considerations to be addressed in planning are to do with balance. This may be balance of approaches or in pedagogies being employed in the school. The major concern is to move away from the 'one size fits all' mentality towards a more considered and clearly enunciated position that values all stakeholders. To rely on just one approach, or on one favoured pedagogy, is to pretend that all students or teachers or schools can benefit from the same treatment. At the heart of every teacher's belief in individual differences lies a valuing of how each person is special in his or her own way. The range of instruments provided offers options to cater for this variance as teachers audit many of the day-to-day decisions that they make about planning in the classroom. These instruments are designed to give teachers the confidence to be able to justify the positions they have taken.

Adamson, A., & Jenson, V. (Directors). (2001). *Shrek* [Motion picture]. United States: DreamWorks SKG & Pacific Data Images.

Anderson, D.K. (Producer), & Doctor, P. (Director). (2001). *Monsters, Inc.* [Motion picture]. United States: Pixar Animated Studios & Walt Disney Pictures.

Anstey, M. (1998). Being explicit about literacy instruction. *Australian Journal of Language and Literacy, 21*(3), 206–221.

Anstey, M. (2002a). It's not all black and white: Postmodern picture books and new literacies. *Journal of Adolescent & Adult Literacy, 45*(6), 444–457.

Anstey, M. (2002b). *Literate futures: Reading.* Coorparoo, Australia: State of Queensland Department of Education.

Anstey, M. (2003). Examining classrooms as sites of literate practice and literacy learning. In G. Bull & M. Anstey (Eds.), *The literacy lexicon* (2nd ed., pp. 103–121). Sydney, NSW: Pearson Education Australia.

Anstey, M., & Bull, G. (2000). *Reading the visual: Written and illustrated children's literature.* Sydney, NSW: Harcourt Australia.

Anstey, M., & Bull, G. (2004). *The literacy labyrinth* (2nd ed.). Sydney, NSW: Pearson Education Australia.

Arizpe, E., & Styles, M. (2003). *Children reading pictures: Interpreting visual texts.* London: Routledge Falmer.

Arnold, H. (1996). Penny plain, tuppence coloured: Reading words and pictures. In V. Watson & M. Styles (Eds.), *Talking pictures* (pp. 164–177). London: Hodder & Stoughton.

Baker, C.D. (1991a). Classroom literacy events. *Australian Journal of Reading, 14*(2), 103–108.

Baker, C.D. (1991b). Literacy practices and social relations in classroom reading events. In C.D. Baker & A. Luke (Eds.), *Towards a critical sociology of reading pedagogy* (pp. 161–188). Philadelphia: John Benjamins.

Baker, C.D., & Freebody, P. (1989a). *Children's first school books: Introductions to the culture of literacy.* Oxford, England: Basil Blackwell.

Baker, C.D., & Freebody, P. (1989b). Talk around text: Constructions of textual and teacher authority in classroom discourse. In S. de Castell, A. Luke, & C. Luke (Eds.), *Language, authority, and criticism: Readings on the school textbook* (pp. 263–283). London: Falmer Press.

Bakhtin, M. (1981). *The dialogic imagination: Four essays.* Houston: University of Texas Press.

Barthes, R. (1975). *S/Z: An essay.* New York: Hill & Wang.

Barton, D. (1994). *Literacy: An introduction to the ecology of written language.* Oxford, England: Blackwell.

Barton, D., Hamilton, M., & Ivanič, R. (Eds). (2000). *Situated literacies: Reading and writing in context.* London: Routledge.

Bondy, E. (1984). Thinking about thinking: Encouraging children's use of metacognitive processes. *Childhood Education, 60*(4), 234–238.

Bradbury, J., Cloonan, A., Essex, G., Giosis, P., Preston, L., Strong, G., et al. (1997). *Teaching reading in the early years*. South Melbourne, Australia: Pearson Education and the Victorian Department of Education, Employment and Training.

Brown, A.L. (1985). *Teaching students to think as they read: Implications for curriculum reform* (Reading Education Rep. No. 58). Urbana: University of Illinois Press.

Brown, A.L., & Kane, M.J. (1988). Preschool children can learn to transfer: Learning to learn and learning from example. *Cognitive Psychology, 20,* 493–523.

Bull, G. (1998). *An interview with Shaun Tan* [Video]. Toowoomba, Australia: University of Southern Queensland Press.

Bull, G. (2003). An investigation of the pedagogy of literature: Using literature to support learning. In G. Bull & M. Anstey (Eds.), *The literacy lexicon* (2nd ed., pp. 145–160). Sydney, NSW: Pearson Education Australia.

Bull, G., & Anstey, M. (2004). The modern picture book. In P. Hunt (Ed.), *International companion encyclopedia of children's literature* (2nd ed., pp. 328–339). London: Routledge.

Cameron, J. (Producer & Director). (1997). *Titanic* [Motion picture]. United States: 20th Century Fox, Paramount Pictures, & Lightstar Entertainment.

Cazden, C.B. (1967). On individual differences in language competence and performance. *Journal of Special Education, 1*(1), 135–150.

Cazden, C.B. (1972). *Child language in education*. New York: Holt, Rinehart & Winston.

Cope, B., & Kalantzis, M. (1995). *Productive diversity: Organizational life in the age of civic pluralism and total globalisation*. Sydney, NSW, Australia: HarperCollins.

Cope, B., & Kalantzis, M. (1997). Putting multiliteracies to the test. *Education Australia, 35,* 17–21.

Cope, B., & Kalantzis, M. (2000). *Multiliteracies: Literacy learning and the design of social futures*. Melbourne, Vic, Australia: Macmillan.

Cope, B., & Kalantzis, M. (2003). *Learning by design*. Altona, Vic, Australia: Common Ground Publishing.

Derrida, J. (1975). The purveyor of truth (W. Domingo, J. Hulbert, M. Ron, & M. Rose-Logan, Trans.). *Yale French Studies, 52,* 31–113.

Doonan, J. (1993). *Looking at pictures in picture books*. Stroud, England: Thimble Press.

Durrant, C., & Green, B. (2000). Literacy and the new technologies in school education: Meeting the l(IT)eracy challenge? *The Australian Journal of Language and Literacy, 23*(2), 89–108.

Edwards-Groves, C. (1999). *Explicit teaching: Focusing teacher talk on literacy* (Primary English Note No. 118). Newtown, NSW, Australia: Primary English Teaching Association.

Edwards-Groves, C. (2003). Building an inclusive classroom through explicit pedagogy: A focus on the language of teaching. In G. Bull & M. Anstey (Eds.), *The literacy lexicon* (2nd ed., pp. 83–101). Sydney, NSW: Pearson Education Australia.

Ellis, E.S. (1986). The role of motivation and pedagogy on the generalization of cognitive strategy training. *Journal of Learning Disabilities, 19*(2), 66–70.

Evans, J. (1998). *What's in the picture? Responding to illustrations in picture books*. London: Paul Chapman Publishing.

Fiske, J. (1987). *Television culture*. London: Routledge.

Fountas, I.C., & Pinnell, G.S. (2001). *Guiding readers and writers, grades 3–6: Teaching comprehension, genre, and content literacy*. Portsmouth, NH: Heinemann.

Freebody, P., Ludwig, C., & Gunn, S. (1995). *Everyday literacy practices in and out of schools in low socioeconomic urban communities* (Vols. 1 & 2). Canberra, Australia: Commonwealth Department of Employment Education and Training.

Freebody, P., & Luke, A. (1990). Literacies programmes: Debates and demands in cultural context. *Prospect: A Journal of Australian TESOL, 5,* 7–16.

Freebody, P., & Luke, A. (2003). Literacy as engaging with new forms of life: The "four roles" model. In M. Anstey & G. Bull (Eds.), *The literacy lexicon* (2nd ed., pp. 51–65). Sydney, NSW: Pearson Education Australia.

Freiberg, J., & Freebody, P. (2001). Re-discovering practical reading activities in schools and homes. *Journal of Research in Reading, 24*(3), 222–234.

French, P., & MacLure, M. (1981). Teachers' questions, pupils' answers: An investigation of questions and answers in the infant classroom. *First Language, 3*(1), 31–45.

Gee, J.P. (1992). *The social mind: Language ideology and social practice.* New York: Bergin & Garvey.

Gee, J.P. (1996). *Social linguistics and literacies: Ideology in discourses.* London: Taylor & Francis.

Goodman, S., & Graddol, D. (Eds.). (1996). *Redesigning English: New texts, new identities.* London: Routledge.

Grieve, A. (1993). Postmodernism in picture books. *Papers, 4*(3), 15–25.

Hagood, M. (2000). New times, new millennium, new literacies. *Reading Research and Instruction, 39*, 311–328.

Hawisher, G.E., & Selfe, C.L. (Eds.) (2000). *Global literacies and the world-wide web.* London: Routledge.

Heap, J.L. (1985). Discourse in the production of classroom knowledge: Reading lesson. *Curriculum Inquiry, 15*(3), 245–279.

Heath, S.B. (1982). Questioning at home and at school: A comparative study. In G. Spindler (Ed.), *Doing the ethnography of schooling* (pp. 103–131). New York: Holt, Rinehart & Winston.

Hornsby, D. (2000). *A closer look at guided reading.* Armadale, Western Australia: Eleanor Curtain.

Howitt, P. (Director). (1998). *Sliding Doors* [Motion picture]. United States: Miramount Films & Paramount Pictures.

Kress, G. (2003). *Literacy in the new media age.* London: Routledge.

Kress, G., & van Leeuwen, T. (1990). *Reading images.* Melbourne, Vic, Australia: Deakin University.

Kress, G., & van Leeuwen, T. (2001). *Multimodal discourse: The modes and media of contemporary communication.* London: Edward Arnold.

Labov, W. (1969). The logic of non-standard English. In N. Keddie (Ed.), *Tinker tailor...the myth of cultural derivation* (pp. 21–66). Melbourne, Vic, Australia: Penguin.

Land, R. (2001). *The Queensland school reform longitudinal study: Teachers' summary.* Brisbane, Australia: The State of Queensland Education Department.

Lankshear, C. (with Gee, P., Knobel, M., & Searle, C.). (1997). *Changing literacies.* Buckingham, England: Open University Press.

Lankshear, C., & Snyder, I. (with Green, B.). (2000). *Teachers and techno-literacies: Managing technology and learning in schools.* Sydney, NSW, Australia: Allen & Unwin.

Lasseter, J. (Director). (1999). *Toy Story 2* [Motion picture]. United States: Pixar Animated Studios & Walt Disney Pictures.

Leadbeater, C. (2000). *Living on thin air: The new economy.* London: Penguin.

Lewis, D. (1990). The constructedness of texts: Picture books and the metafictive. *Signal, 62*, 131–146.

Lewis, D. (2001). *Picturing text: The contemporary children's picturebook.* London: Taylor & Francis.

Lingard, B., Hayes, D., & Mills, M. (2003). Teachers and productive pedagogies: Contextualising, conceptualising, utilising. *Pedagogy, Culture and Society, 11*(3), 399–424.

Lingard, B., Hayes, D., Mills, M., & Christie, P. (2003). *Leading learning: Making hope practical in schools.* Buckingham, England: Open University Press.

Louden, W., & Rivalland, J. (1995). *Literacy at a distance: Literacy learning in distance education*. Perth, WA, Australia: Edith Cowan University.

Ludwig, C., & Herschell, P. (1998). The power of pedagogy: Routines, school literacy practices and outcomes. *The Australian Journal of Language and Literacy, 21*(1), 67–83.

Luke, A. (1993). The social construction of literacy in the primary school. In L. Unsworth (Ed.), *Literacy learning and teaching*. South Melbourne, Vic, Australia: Macmillan.

Luke, A. (1995). When basic skills and information processing aren't enough: Rethinking reading in new times. *Teachers College Record, 97*(1), 95–115.

Luke, A. (2001, July). *How to make literacy policy differently: Generational chance, professionalisation, and literate futures*. Keynote speech presented at the Australian Association of Teachers of English and Australian Literacy Educators' Association Joint National Conference, Hobart, Tas.

Luke, A., & Freebody, P. (1997). Shaping the social practices of reading. In S. Muspratt, A. Luke, & P. Freebody (Eds.), *Constructing critical literacies: Teaching and learning textual practice*. St. Leonards, NSW, Australia: Allen & Unwin.

Luke, A., & Freebody, P. (2000). *Literate futures: Report of the review for Queensland state schools*. Brisbane, Australia: Education Queensland.

Luke, C. (2003). Reading gender and culture in media Discourses. In G. Bull & M. Anstey (Eds.), *The literacy lexicon* (2nd ed., pp. 195–208). Sydney, NSW: Pearson Education Australia.

Mckee, A. (2001). A beginner's guide to textual analysis. *Metro Magazine, 127/128,* 138–149.

McLeod, J.H., Reynolds, R., & Weckert, C. (2001). *Enriching learning*. Katoomba, NSW, Australia: Social Science Press.

Muspratt, S., Luke, A., & Freebody, P. (1997). *Constructing critical literacies: Teaching and learning textual practice*. St. Leonards, NSW, Australia: Allen & Unwin.

New London Group. (1996). A pedagogy of multiliteracies: Designing social futures. *Harvard Educational Review, 66*(1), 60–92.

Nikolajeva, M., & Scott, C. (2001). *How picturebooks work*. New York: Garland.

Nolan, C. (Director). (2000). *Memento* [Motion picture]. United States: Summit Entertainment.

Paris, S.G., Cross, D.R., & Lipson, M.Y. (1984). Informed strategies for learning: A program to improve children's reading awareness and comprehension. *Journal of Educational Psychology, 76*(6), 1239–1252.

Pullman, P. (1989). Invisible pictures. *Signal, 60,* 160–186.

Raimi, S. (Director). (2002). *Spider-Man* [Motion picture]. United States: Columbia Pictures.

Said, E. (1983). *The world, the text, and the critic*. Cambridge, MA: Harvard University Press.

Sinclair, J., & Coulthard, M. (1975). *Towards an analysis of discourse: The language of teachers and pupils*. Oxford, England: Oxford University Press.

Sipe, L.R. (1998). How picture books work: A semiotically framed theory of text-picture relationships. *Literature in Education, 29*(2), 97–108.

Trifonas, P. (1998). Cross-mediality and narrative textual form: A semiotic analysis of the lexical and visual signs and codes in the picture book. *Semiotica, 118*(1/2), 1–70.

Tusting, K. (2000). The new literacy studies and time: An exploration. In D. Barton, M. Hamilton, & R. Ivanič (Eds.), *Situated literacies: Reading and writing in context* (pp. 35–43). London: Routledge.

Unsworth, L. (2002). Changing dimensions of school literacies. *Australian Journal of Language and Literacy, 25*(1), 62–77.

van Leeuwen, T. (1996). Reading B: Moving English, the visual language of film. In S. Goodman & D. Graddol (Eds.), *Redesigning English: New texts, new identities* (pp. 81–105). London: Routledge.

van Leeuwen, T., & Jewitt, C. (2001). *Handbook of visual analysis*. London: Sage.

Watson, V., & Styles, M. (1996). *Talking pictures: Pictorial texts and young readers*. London: Hodder & Stoughton.

Waugh, P. (1984). *Metafiction: The theory and practice of self-conscious fiction*. London: Methuen.

Wilde, L., & Marek, A. (2002). Beyond learning areas: Literacy and the rich-project curriculum. In B. Gordon (Ed.), *Practical literacy programming* (pp. 35–53). Newtown, NSW, Australia: Primary English Teaching Association.

Zammit, K., & Downes, T. (2002). New learning environments and the multiliterate individuals: A framework for educators. *Australian Journal of Language and Literacy, 25*(2), 24–36.

Further Reading

Anstey, M. (1996). Versions of visual literacy. *Proceedings of the 1st National Children's Book Council Conference* (pp. 13–20). Melbourne, Vic, Australia: DW Thorpe.

Anstey, M. (1998). Illustration in children's literature: A creative aesthetic, or a socio-culturally derived text, or both? In R. Pope (Ed.), *Making it real: Proceedings of the 4th Children's Literature Conference* (pp. 37–45). Melbourne, Vic, Australia: Deakin University Press.

Anstey, M. (1998). Illustration in children's literature: Reading multiple discourses. In M. Nimon (Ed.), *Old neighbours, new visions* (pp. 55–67). Adelaide, Australia: University of South Australia Press.

Anstey, M. (2002). *More than cracking the code: Postmodern picture books and new literacies*. In G. Bull & M. Anstey (Eds.), *Crossing the boundaries* (pp. 87–105). Sydney, NSW: Pearson Education Australia.

Bang, M. (1991). *Picture this: How pictures work*. New York: Seastar Books.

Bigum, C., & Green, B. (2003). Literacy education and the new technologies: Hypermedia or media hype? In G. Bull & M. Anstey (Eds.), *The literacy lexicon* (2nd ed., pp. 209–224). Sydney, NSW: Pearson Education Australia.

Bonnici, P. (1998). *Visual language: The hidden medium of communication*. London: Design Fundamentals.

Bull, G. (1995). Children's literature: Using text to construct reality. *Australian Journal of Language and Literacy, 18*(4), 259–269.

Bull, G., & Anstey, M. (Eds.). (2002). *Crossing the boundaries*. Sydney, NSW: Pearson Education Australia.

Bull, G., & Anstey, M. (Eds.). (2003). *The literacy lexicon* (2nd ed.). Sydney, NSW: Pearson Education Australia.

Bull, G., & Anstey, M. (2005). *The literacy landscape*. Sydney, NSW: Pearson Education Australia.

Callow, J. (Ed.). (1999). *Image matters: Visual texts in the classroom*. Newtown, NSW, Australia: Primary English Teaching Association.

Courts, P. (1991). *Literacy and empowerment: The meaning makers*. New York: Bergin & Garvey.

Gee, J.P. (1994). New alignments and old literacies: From fast capitalism to the canon. In B. Shortland-Jones, B. Bosich, & J. Rivalland (Eds.), *Conference papers of the Australian Reading Association Twentieth National Conference* (pp. 1–35). Carlton South, Vic: Australian Reading Association.

Gee, J.P. (2003). Literacy and social minds. In G. Bull & M. Anstey (Eds.), *The literacy lexicon* (2nd ed., pp. 3–14). Sydney, NSW: Pearson Education Australia.

Heap, J.L. (1982). Understanding classroom events: A critique of Durkin, with an alternative. *Journal of Reading Behaviour, 14*(4), 390–411.

Kalantzis, M. (1995). The new citizen and the new state. In W. Hudson (Ed.), *Rethinking Australian citizenship* (pp. 99–110). Sydney, Australia: University of New South Wales Press.

Knobel, M., & Healy, A. (Eds.). (1998). *Critical literacies in the classroom.* Newtown, NSW, Australia: Primary English Teaching Association.

Lankshear, C., & McLaren, P. (1993). *Critical literacy: Politics, praxis and the postmodern.* New York: State University of New York Press.

Lave, J. (1996). Teaching, as learning, in practice. *Mind, Culture, and Activity, 3,* 149–164.

Leu, D.J., & Kinzer, C.K. (2000). The convergence of literacy instruction with networked technologies for information and communication. *Reading Research Quarterly, 35*(1), 108–127.

Luke, A. (1998). Getting over method: Literacy teaching as work in new times. *Language Arts, 75*(4), 305–313.

Luke, A. (2000). Critical literacy in Australia: A matter of context and standpoint. *Journal of Adolescent & Adult Literacy, 43*(5), 448–461.

Luke, A., Comber, B., & Grant, H. (2003). Critical literacies and cultural studies. In G. Bull & M. Anstey (Eds.), *The literacy lexicon* (2nd ed., pp. 15–36). Sydney, NSW: Pearson Education Australia.

Luke, A., & Freebody, P. (1999, August). Further notes on the four resources model. *Reading Online, 3.* Available: http://www.readingonline.org/past/past_index.asp?HREF=/research/lukefreebody.html

Luke, C. (1997). Media literacy and cultural studies. In S. Muspratt, A. Luke, & P. Freebody (Eds.), *Constructing critical literacies: Teaching and learning textual practice* (pp. 19–50). Cresskill, NJ: Hampton Press.

Luke, C. (2001). New times, new media: Where to in media education? *Media International Australia, 101,* 87–100.

Mallan, K. (1999). *In the picture: Perspectives on picture book art and artists.* Wagga Wagga, NSW, Australia: Charles Sturt University Centre for Information Studies.

Nixon, H., & Comber, B. (2001). Film and video bridge popular and classroom cultures. *Journal of Adolescent & Adult Literacy, 44*(5), 480–487.

Nodelman, P. (1988). *Words about pictures: The narrative art of children's picture books.* Athens: University of Georgia Press.

Oliver, N. (1999). *Sand swimmers: The secret life of Australia's dead heart.* Melbourne, Vic, Australia: Lothian.

O'Rourke, M. (2001). Engaging students through ICT: A multiliteracies approach. *Teacher Learning Network, 8*(3), 12–13.

Piore, M., & Sable, C. (1994). *The second industrial divide.* New York: Basic Books.

Sefton-Green, J. (2000). Beyond school: Futures for English and media education. *English in Australia, 127*(8), 14–23.

van Leeuwen, T., & Kress, G. (1995). Critical layout analysis. *Internationale Schulbuchforschung, 17,* 25–43.

CHILDREN'S LITERATURE CITED

Ahlberg, J., & Ahlberg, A. (1986). *The jolly postman: Or other people's letters*. London: Heinemann.

Baillie, A. (1988). *Drac and the gremlin* (J. Tanner, Ill.). Melbourne, Vic, Australia: Viking Kestrel.

Browne, A. (1997). *Willy the dreamer*. London: Walker Books.

Burningham, J. (1977). *Come away from the water, Shirley*. London: Jonathan Cape.

Burningham, J. (1978). *Time to get out of the bath, Shirley*. London: Jonathan Cape.

Crew, G. (1997a). *Tagged* (S. Woolman, Ill.). Adelaide, SA, Australia: Era Publications.

Crew, G. (1997b). *The viewer* (S. Tan, Ill.). Melbourne, Vic, Australia: Lothian.

Macaulay, D. (1990). *Black and white*. Boston: Houghton Mifflin.

Mann, P. (1995). *The frog princess?* (J. Newton, Ill.). London: ABC Books.

Marsden, J. (1998). *The rabbits* (S. Tan, Ill.). Melbourne, Vic, Australia: Lothian.

McLerran, A. (1995). *The ghost dance* (P. Morin, Ill.). New York: Clarion.

Oliver, N. (1999). *Sand Swimmers*. Melbourne, Vic, Australia: Lothian.

Ormerod, J. (1990). *The frog prince*. London: Walker Books.

Planet Dexter. (Ed.). (1999). *This book really sucks! The science behind gravity, flight, leeches, black holes, tornadoes, our friend the vacuum cleaner, and most everything else that sucks*. New York: Author.

Scieszka, J. (1991). *The frog prince continued* (S. Johnson, Ill.). London: Viking.

Sendak, M. (1963). *Where the wild things are*. Melbourne, Vic, Australia: Penguin.

Sendak, M. (1981). *Outside over there*. Melbourne, Vic, Australia: Puffin.

Sendak, M. (1988). *Dear Mili*. Melbourne, Vic, Australia: Puffin.

Wagner, J. (1977). *John Brown, Rose and the midnight cat* (R. Brooks, Ill.). Melbourne, Vic, Australia: Puffin.

Wild, M. (1989). *The very best of friends* (J. Vivas, Ill.). Sydney, NSW, Australia: Margaret Hamilton.

Additional Children's Literature Resources

Postmodern Picture Books

Baillie, A. (1996). *DragonQuest* (W. Harris, Ill.). Gosford, NSW, Australia: Scholastic.

Briggs, R. (1982). *When the wind blows*. London: Penguin.

Browne, A. (1983). *Gorilla*. London: Walker Books.

Browne, A. (1989). *The tunnel*. London: Julia MacRae.

Browne, A. (1992). *Zoo*. London: Random House.

Browne, A. (1997). *Willy the dreamer*. London: Walker Books.

Bunting, E. (1994). *Smoky night* (D. Diaz, Ill.). San Diego, CA: Harcourt Brace Jovanovich.

Crew, G. (1994). *The watertower* (S. Woolman, Ill.). Adelaide, SA, Australia: Era.

Crew, G. (1999). *Memorial* (S. Tan, Ill.). Melbourne, Vic, Australia: Lothian.

French, F. (1986). *Snow White in New York*. Oxford, England: Oxford University Press.

Hathorn, L. (1994). *Way home* (G. Rogers, Ill.). Sydney, NSW, Australia: Random House.

Scieszka, J. (1989). *The true story of the 3 little pigs* (L. Smith, Ill.). Melbourne, Vic, Australia: Puffin.

Scieszka, J. (1992). *The stinky cheese man and other fairly stupid tales* (L. Smith, Ill.). Melbourne, Vic, Australia: Viking Penguin.

Multiple Versions of Stories

Cinderella

Cole, B. (1986). *Princess Smartypants*. London: Collins.

Cole, B. (1987). *Prince Cinders*. London: Hamish Hamilton.

Craft, K.Y. (2000). *Cinderella*. New York: Seastar Books.

French, F. (1987). *Cinderella*. Oxford, England: Oxford University Press.

Glitz, A., & Swoboda, A. (2001). *Prince Charming and Baabarella*. London: Cats Whiskers.

Resnick, J. (1990). *Cinderella*. Westport, CT: Joshua Morris.

Storey, R. (1991). *Cinderella*. Ringwood, Vic, Australia: Puffin.

Noah Stories

Auch, M.J. (1999). *Noah's aardvark*. New York: Golden Books.

Chapman, J. (1988). *Blue gum ark*. Sydney, NSW, Australia: Ashton Scholastic.

Holder, M. (2004). *All safe on board*. Oxford, England: Lion Hudson.

Janisch, H. (1997). *Noah's ark*. New York: North South Books.

Joslin, M. (1999). *The tale of the Heaven tree*. Oxford, England: Lion.

Lee, H. (1986). *The story of Noah's ark*. London: Tiger Books.

Miyoshi, S. (1985). *What happened in the ark?* London: Dent.

Randall, R. (2003). *Noah's ark*. Bath, England: Paragon.

Rothero, C. (1994). *Noah and the ark*. London: Award Publications.

Wildsmith, B. (1980). *Professor Noah's spaceship*. Oxford, England: Oxford University Press.

The Selfish Giant

Foreman, M., & Wright, F. (1978). *The selfish giant*. Ringwood, Vic, Australia: Puffin.

Laslett, S. (retold by). (1994). *The selfish giant*. London: Paragon.

Mansell, D. (1986). *The selfish giant*. London: Walker Books.

Waters, F., & Negrin, F. (1999). *The selfish giant*. London: Bloomsbury.

Zwerger, L. (1994). *The selfish giant*. London: North South Books.

INDEX

Note. Page numbers followed by *f* and *t* indicate figures and tables, respectively.